calm
handbook

A
Communal
Approach to
Learning
Meditation

by

Paul Profaska

George Ronald
Oxford

George Ronald, *Publisher*
www.grbooks.com

*A catalogue record for this book is available
from the British Library*

ISBN 0–85398–493–x

to the CALM course
for what will hopefully be an
uplifting and inspiring journey of discovery for you

It is very heartening to know that an increasing number of people are exploring and promoting meditation, for it is so vitally important for both our personal well-being and that of humanity as a whole.

The writings of all spiritual traditions affirm to us that as human beings we have a most wondrous potential – a capacity to be filled with spiritual qualities and insights, which in turn will enable us to live our lives more fully and meaningfully.

Meditation is one of the essential skills we need to learn if we are to develop this potential and one of the main aims of the CALM course is to create an environment where we can experience a profound sense of peacefulness and learn to connect more effectively with this inner spiritual nature.

No particular form of meditation is promoted but several meditation exercises are used to enable us to experience the different stages of the meditation process, explore the relevant principles involved at each stage, develop our own practice and consider how it could help us in our lives.

The CALM course is designed so that people from different spiritual backgrounds and walks of life can come together in an atmosphere of mutual respect as co-learners of meditation. Rather than exploring what we believe, we will be focusing on developing our understanding of the experience, principles and practice of meditation, which are becoming more widely accepted and are common to all. Although the CALM course approaches meditation from a perspective based on the Bahá'í writings, the basic principles are common to all traditions and it would add to the richness of the CALM course if participants felt able to share contributions from the literature of their own backgrounds. We ask, though, that any readings brought are short and focused on whatever is relevant at the time, to keep the meetings uncomplicated and experiential rather than overly intellectual.

The CALM course runs for nine two-hour meetings. Each meeting has a similar format, starting with some time to say hello and to feed back anything you would like to share with the group. After settling down there will be a guided meditation, followed by a period of silence. Towards the end of this silence there is a very short reading relevant to the topic being focused on that day. Then there will be a chance to feed back your thoughts about the meditation and to explore the day's topic. Finally, there is time for refreshments and socializing.

For everyone to benefit from the CALM course, and for meetings to work well, it is very helpful if the *CALM Handbook* is studied prior to each meeting. Read section 1 before meeting 1, and so on. You will also find it helpful to have the *CALM Handbook* with you at meetings.

Everyone on the CALM course, including the coordinator(s) uses the *CALM Handbook*. You will find that each section of the *Handbook* is divided into three parts:

Part 1: Helpful information to be studied before the meeting

Part 2: The programme for use during the meeting

Part 3: Suggested personal practice for between meetings

The information in part 1 does not presume to be the only point of view but it will help you to be better prepared for the next meeting.

Much of part 2 is intended for the coordinator of the meeting and it is not essential that everyone read it or involve themselves in following its details at meetings. Including it here empowers everyone equally and means that you could even take on running part of a meeting, if this is something you would like to try. If you would like to do this, it is preferable if you consult about it with whoever is running the course well before the meeting.

The parts on personal practice will be more meaningful once the CALM course has started. There is also an appendix containing helpful information.

Furthering our understanding of the faculty of meditation and learning to apply its benefits to life are processes in which we are all learners. With all of the challenges that face us, both individually and collectively, there has never been a more important time for us to learn to draw upon our inner strengths, not just to help us deal with the problems but also to take advantage of all the wondrous possibilities that life in this new age offers.

Lastly, feel reassured that all of us have the capacity to live life more fully. Take the CALM course as an opportunity for new doors to be opened to you. Making changes to the patterns of our life is a challenge but whatever we enjoy practising we will get better at. The people who have got the most benefit from the CALM course are those who sensed that meditation would bring greater well-being into their lives and made the commitment for just a few weeks.

Wishing you confirmations with your efforts and a bountiful journey of discovery.

Contents

Words fall so far short when trying to describe that mystic feeling which is the essence of meditation and prayer. In the inter-faith meditation groups we have run in Cornwall over the past 30 years people have, in their attempt to do so, described their experiences as one of profound peacefulness; of being connected with God, with the Source; at one with everything; reaching a deeper level of consciousness; coming home, or returning to their real self; of being filled with love or gaining insights into life's issues, and of experiencing deep bonds of fellowship with others in the group.

Over the years, promoting and supporting these meetings was a cherished part of my life, so when in 1999 the National Assembly of the Bahá'ís of the United Kingdom offered me the opportunity to set up a pilot project for promoting the use of meditation I was very enthusiastic about it.

Here was a chance to promote something that not only enables us to discover and connect with our spiritual nature and find an inner source of comfort and strength but also helps release our potential to contribute more effectively towards the well-being of all.

The possibilities of such a project attracted a number of Bahá'ís and brought their diverse abilities and backgrounds into a pilot committee. Over the course of a year, and using meditation as part of our consultation process, we explored what the Bahá'í teachings say about the subject and how meditation could best be promoted. In the end we chose to develop a meditation course because, although it is relatively easy to create a situation where meditation can be experienced, to integrate its benefits into daily life requires the gaining of some insight into the process and regular practice.

What was developed was a safe, straightforward introductory course on meditation that was suitable for people from all backgrounds, facilitated the experience of meditation, gave an understanding of its basic principles, developed skills that provided a basis for subsequent practice and explored its practical benefits and applications. The next step was to try it out with our friends locally.

What I was doing came up in general conversation with a friend who lived in a nearby town. She was keen to have a course there, so it was left that if she could find the people we would run a course. Somewhat to my surprise she telephoned the next day to say that she had a group who were interested. What had happened was that she had belonged to a women's support group for a couple of years and they had recently begun to feel that they wanted to move on in some way. The meditation course provided such an opportunity.

I was inspired by the thought of running a course but also felt some trepidation at the thought of having to relate to a well-integrated and empowered group of women. However, they were easy to be with. What most of them were hoping for from the course was to be able to manage their mental over-activity rather than seeing it as some sort of spiritual development.

One of them, in particular, was quite highly strung, dominated the conversation and had a skin complaint on her legs which she found it necessary to scratch quite often. I found it hard to muster any faith that the course might actually work for her but although she did not feel any benefits herself, she tried hard and stuck with us, perhaps encouraged by some positive feedback from the others of how they were getting on. In our fifth meeting I thought she had fallen asleep during the meditation so we began the feedback and discussion without her. Then, after about ten minutes, she opened her eyes and, calmly and with great feeling said, 'I understand what this is about now.'

She had connected with that calm inner centre of comfort, insight and strength which religious traditions affirm is within us all. I came away from the meeting quite overtaken with the feeling of what a great privilege it was to be part of this process of transformation.

Once we had run several pilot courses and made many modifications we began to provide week-long facilitators' workshops in which we trained others who felt they would like to set up courses in their own areas. The workshops were inspiring, fun and a great learning experience for all involved but the crucial question was, 'Would people manage to run a meditation course afterwards?' Some of the group members were very capable people, sometimes with a background in meditation, but what was subsequently heartening to see was that people who lacked confidence and had no significant previous experience of meditation were able to run effective courses.

One difficulty we faced in furthering the project was that the people who were interested in participating were widely scattered around the country, which meant it cost time and money to get together and it was not possible to meet everyone's needs. During one of these facilitator's workshops I became unwell and my wife had to take over. Though she had been involved in a couple of meditation courses she had not run this workshop and had to do so unprepared and using my notes. I just sat and watched it happening but what became apparent was that it would be possible to modify the course in such a way that anyone who wished to could run a meditation course without training but with the right materials.

So yet again the course was improved and modified, and some trial courses were run. What resulted is the present programme, the Communal Approach to Learning Meditation (CALM), an easy-to-follow and effective approach to learning meditation for people happy to work together in small groups.

1

Why Meditate?

MOTIVATION

In the first meeting we will be looking at motivation – what we think the benefits of meditation could be and in what way we feel meditation could help us.

Whatever motivates our hearts and minds is a key factor in opening the doors of our future; with motivation we can make choices and grow. We should at least be open to the possibility that there are treasures within us that meditation can help us discover.

Think about why you are joining the CALM course and what you hope to get from it. If you feel like it, you could share these thoughts with everyone when we get together.

A HELPFUL MODEL

The Sun and the Mirror

The most important part of the first session, and of every session, is having the opportunity to experience and share meditation together. If you have very little or no previous involvement with meditation, the following model provides a mental picture of how it works. It is like a map which, although it is not the real world, still helps us to understand where we are going and enables us to feel more in control.

Many traditions use the analogy that God or the Divine Essence or our Higher Self can be compared to the sun and our souls or minds are like mirrors that can receive and reflect its light, in the form of love or understanding.

In one sense meditation is that simple – turning the mirror of our consciousness towards this inner light – but generally life has taught us to be more complicated and made it more difficult. Even if we believe there is an inner source of comfort and strength and are willing to look inside ourselves to try and find it, our consciousness tends to be filled with so much activity, sensations, emotions and patterns of thinking that our ability to see and experience the treasures that are potentially always there is blocked.

In addition, the ability to concentrate our attention in one direction is, generally, underdeveloped, so after a few seconds of trying, sounds, thoughts or emotions distract us and seem to frustrate our efforts to find the light within. This is where we can make things easier for ourselves by using an appropriate meditation technique. Step by step, gently each day, we can all change our lives – if we choose to.

BEING STILL

Developing a sense of inner stillness is one of the first things we need to attend to. Taking forward the analogy of the mirror and the sun, if we think of a pond, it is in some ways like a mirror. When the water is still it can reflect the image of the sky and the plants around its edge and be warmed by the sun.

If we think of our consciousness as being like this pond, we have the capacity to receive and reflect understanding and have the potential to be warmed by the experience of beautiful qualities such as profound peace, love, courage and so on.

If we wanted to study the reflections in a pond we would not get a stick and poke around in it, for that would create waves and stir up sediment that would obscure what we could see. But when we want to look into our inner self and meditate, that is what we tend to do. The waves and sediment are our thoughts and emotions that have already been stirred up and the stick is our ego's active efforts to be in control of the investigation, which only makes matters worse.

If we can learn to hold the stick of our mind's investigative faculties still and let ourselves, initially, become open and receptive, just to witness, the thoughts and emotions will settle down and we will become enchanted by the beauty within. Many meditation techniques help us to do this by focusing our attention on one thing at a time.

THE USE OF FOCUSING

This leads us to another issue. It is not normal for most of us to be able to focus our attention in a meditative way for more than a few seconds before sounds from the world around us or thoughts and feelings from the world within us disturb our concentration. Meditation techniques that use some form of focusing as part of their practice are trying to help us with this problem. They teach us to become more still inside by just concentrating repeatedly for a few seconds at a time. Holding the stick still, even for a short while, over and over again, allows the disturbance in the pond to settle.

AVOIDING FRUSTRATION

When, as is inevitable, sounds, thoughts or feelings creep into our practice it is completely counterproductive to get frustrated by them. This frustration has the same effect as angrily thrashing the stick in the pond – it just stirs everything up.

We can learn to work with, not fight with, ourselves, by noticing when we have become distracted, just observing what has distracted us, then letting it go – and getting right back to whatever we are focusing on. This is central to the work of uncluttering our consciousness so that it is ready to experience the benefits of meditation.

MEDITATION DURING THE CALM COURSE

The meditation periods during the CALM course are all similar, except that we take on more responsibility for our own practice as the weeks go by and we also begin to explore how meditation can help us manage our lives better.

The way we are going to practise meditation at first is by following a recording of a guided meditation but this may change as the CALM course progresses and everyone feels more confident.

What this guided meditation will be taking us through is a series of very easy focusing exercises, similar to those used by all religions for thousands of years. These will help to settle our thoughts and make us more receptive to feeling a sense of peaceful well-being and love or whatever feels right for us that day.

To do this we do not have to remember any previous instructions or have had any experience. All we need to do is to want to feel better inside and follow the directions given with the same amount of trust that we might have if a friend were taking us on a walk in some beautiful countryside that we had never explored before.

One important thing to remember when we are practising is what to do when our minds are distracted by sounds around us or things inevitably wander into our thoughts. Once we become aware of whatever it is, just follow these simple steps:

- **Name** what you are experiencing – car sound, dog barking, thought, daydream.

- **Focus** on it briefly, experience it for what it is.

- **Return** to the practice, again and again, without any frustration, about having become distracted.

In this way everything becomes part of the meditation rather than working against it. (We will be reminded about this during the meditation.)

Then, after the guided meditation, there is about five minutes silence for personal reflection.

HOW WE SHARE OUR THOUGHTS AND FEELINGS

After the first meditation there will be a period for sharing thoughts and feelings about the meditation. In later meetings this is also a time to explore whatever is that session's topic.

Having the freedom and opportunity to share our understandings and feelings is an essential ingredient of the group, so when we are communicating could we try to:

- regard it more as an opportunity to listen than to speak
- think of people's thoughts as prayers – avoid criticizing them
- do not feel obliged to speak but remember your viewpoint is important
- forgive ourselves and others when we fall short

It will be helpful to use a model something like this for our discussions because it will:

- help us to learn to cultivate an inner meditative attitude at the same time as dealing with outer affairs (this is one way we can apply meditation to life)
- help us to learn to listen more sensitively to others' thoughts and feelings
- enable us to learn more from each other

DEVELOPING A COMMON UNDERSTANDING

With a group of people from different backgrounds there is always the possibility that the sort of language we use can become a barrier to communication; we may use words like 'God', 'spirit', 'higher self', 'deeper level of consciousness' in an attempt to describe our inner experiences. As we listen to each other hopefully we will come to understand what we each mean when language is used that is different from ours and have respect for the way other people describe their experiences.

We are getting together for an inner journey to explore this wonderful capacity to meditate that we all have. Using the model of the sun and the mirror again, it is surely more important that, as a group, we experience the light than argue about its source.

To help with our understanding of each other there will be, if you want, an opportunity during the first meeting to share our thoughts about the terminology we use to describe our experiences of the inner world. For example, would you describe your efforts to get into a state of meditation as helping you to feel closer to God or bringing you into a deeper state of consciousness?

Also, because people in the group come from different backgrounds, to avoid the risk of disharmony, we will avoid talking about our beliefs, at least while the sessions are in progress, and we will focus on developing our understanding of meditation.

PERSEVERANCE

During life we put a great amount of effort into learning certain things – studying for exams, training for work, learning to drive. Being able to meditate is arguably more important for our well-being and progress than any of these, so we need to have confidence that meditation can help us in many ways and that whatever we enjoy practising we will get better at.

Sometimes people have inspiring and confirming experiences during meditation. Other times meditation can be less fulfilling or even frustrating and we need to discover what the obstacles are. Sometimes we can even uncover things that are painful to deal with or, as we become more self-aware, may feel that we are becoming a worse person.

Whether we continue to investigate meditation or not, there are consequences of our choice but if we wish to liberate ourselves from those parts of us that limit our ability to draw upon the spiritual resources we all have, we owe it to ourselves to persevere in a nurturing, self-caring way. This will be looked at in more detail later in the CALM course.

It is such a pleasure to be with people who are endeavouring to cultivate greater well-being, both for the benefit of ourselves and for those around us. Thank you for reading this. Hopefully it will have prepared you to get more out of the first meeting.

MAIN AIMS OF THIS MEETING

To explore why meditation is of such great value to us.

For everyone to get a feel for meditation.

PRACTICAL POINTS FOR RUNNING THE MEETING

The Role of the Coordinator

The CALM course is designed for groups of people who wish to co-learn meditation as equals. For meetings to work there needs to be a coordinator responsible for ensuring certain things happen.

Instructions to assist coordinators are included in the programme for each meeting.

Depending on the preference of each group there might be one person running the whole CALM course or several members of the group taking it in turns to run meetings or parts of meetings.

The programme indicates where the coordinator has a responsibility, for example, welcoming everyone, asking questions, initiating and ending meditations and consultations.

The coordinator should also, of course, contribute to all sharing and consultation.

Hello Time

Particularly with this first session, if the 'Hello' time is allowed to go on for too long or become unfocused, it is liable to have a detrimental effect on the meditation that follows.

A balance needs to be struck between the sharing of thoughts and feelings and raising questions without over-activating or cluttering minds prior to meditating.

CDs

Some people have very much appreciated having a recording of the guided meditation to help with their practice at home and this is supplied with this book.

WELCOME AND INTRODUCING OURSELVES

Coordinator

Briefly welcome everyone to the exciting spiritual journey of discovery you are to share together.

Ensure everyone in the circle can see each other as best as possible, circumstances permitting, and that people are comfortable and not cramped together. Also check to see if everyone can hear what is being said.

SHARING THOUGHTS IN A CIRCLE (VOLUNTARY)

Coordinator

Invite the group to introduce themselves, if necessary, going around in the circle.

Possible question:

Would you like to introduce yourself and let us know how you feel meditation could benefit you?

Summarize why meditation is beneficial (e.g. because we have the capacity to experience life more richly and live it more fully – uplifts heart, illumines mind, improves concentration and awareness, develops self-control, relaxes body, reduces stress, promotes healing, etc.).

INTRODUCE MEDITATION

Coordinator

Provide information if necessary and initiate settling down.

Possible questions:

Section 1 in the *CALM Handbook* is meant to give us some idea about how meditation works. Was it helpful?

Is there anything you would like to bring up or clarify?

The way we are going to practise meditation is by following a recorded guided meditation. This may change as the CALM course progresses but today we are going to listen to the recording.

After the guided meditation there will be about five minutes' silence.

Any comments or questions?

SETTLING DOWN

Switch off/unplug phones, use the toilet, etc. Settle into silence with some music.

MEDITATION PERIOD
MEDITATION

Coordinator

Initiate guided meditation using the CD from track 5.

Follow the end of the guided meditation with a five minute period of silence.

Then to bring the meditation period to a close suggest:

> Could we all bring our attention back into the room now and focus on our feet resting firmly on the ground. (Give people a minute to readjust.)

> Thank you all for contributing towards that experience. It would be of benefit to us if we could practise staying with some of the feeling of our meditation, as we move on now, so we can share our feelings and thoughts in an atmosphere of consideration and mindfulness.

FEEDBACK
Coordinator

Invite voluntary feedback about meditation, taking turns around the circle.

Possible questions:

> Has anybody anything they'd like to share about how the meditation went for them?

> How did you get on with keeping your mind focused during the breathing exercise?

> How did the period of silence feel? Was it too long or too short?

Note:

- Identify problems as opportunities for growth – becoming aware of the thoughts, etc. that enter our consciousness is part of learning to meditate.
- Let people identify what they feel their obstacle is and how they might try to overcome it.

Common areas that require attention are:

- Enhanced motivation and commitment – by recognizing meditation's immense value to us.
- The need for regular practice – we will improve.
- Adopting a nurturing attitude to personal growth – not forcing things.

CONSULTATION

Coordinator

Initiate consultation about the next two topics.

How We Consult

Learning to make listening to each other part of the meditative experience.

Possible question:

> Without being rigid, when we are sharing our thoughts, can we try to take turns speaking, going around the circle to give everyone who wants to a chance to contribute. How do you feel about this?

Developing a Common Understanding

A factor that can make communication difficult is misunderstanding what particular words or phrases mean to different people.

Possible question:

> There are different ways in which we could describe our efforts to get into a state of meditation: helping us to feel closer to God or getting into a deeper state of consciousness. How would you describe what you are trying to do when you meditate?

CONCLUDE

Wish everyone well with their personal practice.

Are there any comments or questions?

SOCIALIZE

Milk and sugar?

Hopefully the first meeting of the CALM Meditation course was of benefit to you.

In the meeting we looked at some of the benefits to be had from meditation and, if we would like to become more fulfilled and happy beings in the longer term, how one of the most important things we need to do is to practise becoming that way.

We have all spent years unconsciously practising and rehearsing both the positive and negative attitudes, moods and responses that have become part of us and while it is relatively easy to feel like a different, more positive, person while we are meditating, it is not necessarily easy to carry those more peaceful, loving, inspired feelings back into our lives. Once we leave the sanctuary of the meditation group it is so easy to just slip back into the way we are.

So, if we want to change something about ourselves, it is important that we practise regularly the new qualities we would like to have in our lives. What we practise we get better at; especially if it is a positive, encouraging experience.

We have all learned to do complicated things in our lives, like riding a bike, writing or playing an instrument; and while doing these things initially took an effort, eventually, with practice, they became second nature and we could do them without thinking. Of course, it helped if we enjoyed what we practised.

Why not practise with the relaxation and breathing exercise that we used in the session, especially if you do not have some form of regular meditative activity. It does not matter if you do the exercise a bit differently or modify it to suit your needs. Do not underestimate the contribution these simple exercises can make towards empowering you. If you do have some form of regular meditative activity just see if it makes a difference to use the first step below – asking yourself why you are doing it and making a commitment.

Be gentle with yourself at first: a little effective practice is better than getting into the habit of bad practice. Look in the section 'Helpful Tips about Practising Meditation' at the end of the *CALM Handbook* about when, where and how long to meditate. Be positive about your efforts. If you have managed to take one breath mindfully, that's better than none and it is a new beginning.

It will help to remember these things:

- Just before you start ask your self why you are doing it (because you want to be a more joyful, peaceful, mindful being or whatever) and commit yourself to it – it is, after all, beneficial for you.

- Learn to allow yourself to just be with, and take an interest in, the experience of the relaxation or breathing exercise.

- Once you are aware that you have become distracted by sounds around you, or wandered into thoughts:

    - **Name** what you are experiencing – car sound, dog barking, thought, daydream.
    - **Focus** on it briefly to experience it for what it is.
    - **Return** to the practice **without any frustration**, about having become distracted, again and again.

In this way everything becomes part of the meditation rather than working against it.

2

What is Meditation?

There are so many different views about what meditation is. For the CALM course to effectively cover the fundamentals of meditation in such a short period and give everyone a foundation for future practice we need to be working in the same direction. To help this happen meditation is approached in a particular way – which is, in fact, similar to the way many people approach it. This does not imply that other approaches to meditation are of less value.

MEDITATION IN THE CONTEXT OF THE CALM COURSE

Though developing our own understanding of meditation is a part of the CALM course, we can all learn something from the perspectives of others; so sharing our points of view will be part of what we are doing during the next meeting.

To do this, meeting 2 explores and identifies the principles that underlie what is understood as 'meditation', so that, hopefully, we will be able to understand each other better.

Often meditation is thought of in the context of how it is used, so you could think of meditation as just being about relaxation or healing or mindfulness or spiritual growth, etc.

Meditation is sometimes associated with the exercises, or practices, that we use to help us move into a state of meditation but doing the exercises does not necessarily mean we are meditating.

The perspective from which we will be exploring meditation is the belief that we all have the capacity to move into a special, deeper state of consciousness in which our hearts and minds can be illumined, bringing tangible benefits to both ourselves and others in many ways.

So we could be in a state of meditation

> sitting at home, alone or with others, connected to the 'spiritual realms' and becoming uplifted and inspired with great insights.

Or we could, in a state of meditation be

> walking in the countryside, running a marathon, listening to music, painting a picture, solving a difficult problem or listening mindfully at a committee meeting.

Of course, the more effectively we practise, the more likely this is to be the case!

HOW WE STUDY

In the coming meetings we are going to begin our exploration of what meditation is and what it means to us. There are two important aspects of this:

- One is what we experience, what we feel it to be.

- The other is theoretical, what we think it is.

The experiential part involves the exploration and discoveries we make about our inner selves, the challenges we come across and the sense of peace we tune into, the insights or healing, or whatever we get, and the inner skills we develop. These experiences are the essence of the CALM course and could be thought of as being like the individual parts of a jigsaw, very real, important and fascinating in themselves.

The theoretical part deals with the principles and practice of meditation. This will help us to apply and incorporate what we have learned into our lives. In the CALM course the theory is based on the Bahá'í writings but you are welcome to share any other material you may think we would find helpful. As you may have found yourself, these principles and teachings are universal and people of all faiths and disciplines have promoted them. This theoretical part is, in a sense, like the larger picture of the completed jigsaw puzzle, against which we can compare our little pieces, explore the broader picture and develop our own understandings.

One of the ways we are going to use the Bahá'í writings is this. In each session, towards the end of the silent part of our meditation, a short passage that is relevant to the stage of meditation we are exploring will be read. Listening mindfully to this is one way we can learn to apply meditation to help us gain greater insight into the different issues of life. Then, when the meditation is concluded, we will go on to share our thoughts and feelings about it and explore other aspects of the day's focus using other writings.

Whoever is coordinating the meeting may ask others to share the reading with them, so if you would rather not read you could point this out at some stage before the meeting.

MAIN AIMS OF THIS MEETING

To explore what meditation means to us.

To clarify the perspective from which meditation is being approached in the CALM course.

PRACTICAL POINTS FOR RUNNING THE MEETING

FEEDBACK ABOUT PERSONAL PRACTICE

How people get on will vary quite a bit. Some will practise regularly and get a lot out of it, others will find it a big challenge and some may not really want to practise yet and will prefer just to meditate with the group.

Points to remember are:

- whatever we practise we get better at, and
- we should make our practice something we look forward to
- because it will be of great benefit to us and
- if we keep it up we will feel the difference.

SHARING OUR VIEWS

With regard to the consultation period, how rigid or flexible this is depends on the coordinator and the group but some points are:

- we are trying to deepen our understanding of our inner world, learning to listen to what could be called the inner voice of the Spirit, so allowing freedom of expression is important but
- if the focus contained in the quotations is lost, the group's progress will be hampered, so
- we are trying to strike a balance between learning with the heart and learning with the head

To bring this about the coordinator could

- encourage the sharing of views by going round the circle
- keep people focused by asking them to respond to a particular point in the quotation
- welcome everyone's point of view but if it is leading off track, let the person finish his or her point (provided they are not going on at length)
- then refocus the group by asking the next person to speak to the subject being dealt with

HELLO TIME

Coordinator

Allow an appropriate period of time for people to say hello and chat.

Focus the group.

Taking turns round the circle, ask the group how they have got on since the last meeting.

Possible questions:

Did anyone attempt to practise?

How did it go?

Invite people to share any contributions of writings, poetry or thoughts that relate to the last meeting.

Coordinator

Inform/remind the group of today's focus, if necessary:

> Today we are going to explore what meditation means to us, and also clarify the perspective from which meditation is approached in the CALM course.
>
> Any questions/comments?

SETTLING DOWN

Switch off/unplug phones, use the toilet, etc. Settle into silence with some music.

MEDITATION PERIOD
MEDITATION

Coordinator

Play the CD starting from track 6: '*So, sitting comfortably and upright, with our eyes closed, breathing naturally, let's begin.*'

Towards the end of the five minute period of silence that follows the meditation read this passage:

> *Meditation is the key for opening the doors of mysteries. In that state man abstracts himself: in that state man withdraws himself from all outside objects; in that subjective mood he is immersed in the ocean of spiritual life and can unfold the secrets of things-in-themselves.*
> *The meditative faculty is akin to the mirror; if you put it before earthly objects it will reflect them. Therefore if the spirit of man is contemplating earthly subjects he will be informed of these.*
> *But if you turn the mirror of your spirits heavenwards, the heavenly constellations and the rays of the Sun of Reality will be reflected in your hearts, and the virtues of the Kingdom will be obtained.*[1]

Allow a short while for reflection, then bring the meditation period to a close:

> Could we all bring our attention back into the room now and focus our attention on our feet resting firmly on the ground. (Give people a minute to readjust.)

FEEDBACK
Coordinator

Thank the group for participating in the meditation and invite the sharing of feedback.

Possible questions:

- Is there anything about the meditation you'd like to share with us?
- Did any particular thoughts come to you?

Give the group an opportunity to share their thoughts about what meditation is.

What does meditation mean to you?

Give everyone a chance to contribute but avoid a long debate otherwise there will not be time to study the CALM course perspective.

CONSULTATION

TODAY'S FOCUS – WHAT IS MEDITATION?

Coordinator

Introduce today's focus and initiate consultation.

Read and discuss quotations in a manner that suits the group – e. g.

- Invite others to share the reading (best to check with people privately first).
- Read one quotation at a time, asking questions about each one; repeat if required.
- Everyone make up their own questions and/or use those provided.
- Keep the focus.

Quotations

Meditation is the key for opening the doors of mysteries. In that state man abstracts himself: in that state man withdraws himself from all outside objects; in that subjective mood he is immersed in the ocean of spiritual life and can unfold the secrets of things-in-themselves.[2]

The meditative faculty is akin to the mirror; if you put it before earthly objects it will reflect them. Therefore if the spirit of man is contemplating earthly subjects he will be informed of these.
But if you turn the mirror of your spirits heavenwards, the heavenly constellations and the rays of the Sun of Reality will be reflected in your hearts, and the virtues of the Kingdom will be obtained.[3]

Through the faculty of meditation man attains to eternal life; through it he receives the breath of the Holy Spirit – the bestowal of the Spirit is given in reflection and meditation.
The spirit of man is itself informed and strengthened during meditation; through it affairs of which man knew nothing are unfolded before his view. Through it he receives Divine inspiration, through it he receives heavenly food.[4]

This faculty brings forth from the invisible plane the sciences and arts. Through the meditative faculty inventions are made possible, colossal undertakings are carried out; through it governments can run smoothly.[5]

DEFINITION

Faculty: An ability, aptitude or competence for a particular kind of action (as with the faculty of speech); a personal quality; disposition; an inherent power or property of the body or an organ or the mind (such as memory, reason, etc.); a physical capability.[6]

Possible Questions

Quotation 1

- What are some of the words or phrases this passage uses to describe what meditation is?
- What are some of the things that we need to do to enter a state of meditation?
- In today's meditation, what did we do that helped us 'withdraw' from the world?

Quotation 2

- Any thoughts on what the term 'meditative faculty' could mean?
- What does the passage tell us about the faculty of meditation?

Quotation 3

- What are some of the personal benefits of meditation identified here?

Quotation 4

- What are some of the other possible applications of meditation?

SUMMARY

Coordinator

So, the perspective from which meditation is being approached in the CALM course is that

- all human beings can access a very special, receptive state of consciousness that 'Abdu'l-Bahá describes as our faculty of meditation

- when we are using our faculty of meditation we are meditating or in a meditative state

- in this meditative state our hearts are receptive to empowerment with spiritual qualities, such as love, and our minds can be awakened with insight and wisdom

- meditation is not an end in itself but part of a process through which the illumination of our hearts and minds can bring tangible benefits to both ourselves and others in many ways

Question:

- Is this an approach that everyone can work with?

Invite comments.

CONCLUDE

Coordinator

Anything else to share?

SOCIALIZE

In meeting 2 we looked at what meditation is and identified the perspective from which it is being approached in the CALM course, which is that:

- all human beings can access a very special, receptive state of consciousness which 'Abdu'l-Bahá describes as the faculty of meditation

- just as when we use our faculty of sight we are seeing, when we use our faculty of meditation we are meditating, or in a meditative state

- in this meditative state our hearts are receptive to being empowered with spiritual qualities such as love, and our minds can be awakened with insight and wisdom

- meditation is not an end in itself but part of a process through which the illumination of our hearts and minds can bring tangible benefits to both ourselves and others in many ways

'Abdu'l-Bahá affirmed that all human beings have this special capacity to experience life, and live it, so much more fully through use of our 'meditative faculty'. One of the things we are doing in this CALM course is investigating this for ourselves. We are all somewhere along the often challenging, ultimately bountiful, journey of opening up to our hidden potential.

So for our own sakes, let's keep up some practice and, if necessary, revisit the helpful advice in the 'Personal Practice' at the end of meeting 1 or in appendix 1. Evaluate what you are doing and be open to being inspired with your own ways of making your practice more satisfying and effective.

The affirmation used at the beginning of the meditation is to help make it easier for us to withdraw our attention from the outside world. It brings us into the here and now by asking us to look at why we are bothering to meditate and to find a heartfelt reason for doing so. This also helps to prevent our meditation practice from becoming an unconscious ritual. We are also invited to consider our intentions – whether there is anything that could be more important for our souls than what we are doing right now and, if not, to commit ourselves to the meditation.

Bearing in mind that what we think we might want from a meditation may change as we go into it, identifying a personal affirmation for the day can also be a useful tool for refocusing ourselves when the mind wanders off into daydreams and so on during our practice.

One of this meeting's quotations states that to 'withdraw from all outside objects' is part of the process of entering the state of meditation and this is why the relaxation exercise is used. As well as helping us to release tension, it is a useful tool for helping us to 'withdraw' from the outside world and focus our attention within our bodies. Any relaxation exercise that suits us could be used and need not necessarily take a long time to perform.

3

Principles of Meditation

In this meeting we will be looking at the basic principles of how meditation works. These were introduced in the first section of this *Calm Handbook* to provide a mental picture of what we are trying to do when we meditate, using analogies about the sun and the mirror, the pond and the stick.

This time we will be exploring these principles again, comparing them with our experience of meditation so far and taking them a bit further. All this will help us to understand why certain aspects of practice are so important for helping us to develop our meditation and bring its benefits into our lives.

Part of our role in learning to develop our ability to meditate is being able to recognize those things that come between us and our feeling happier and more fulfilled. During the meditation period this time, to help us listen to our intuition and know ourselves better, we will practice what could be called 'listening with the heart'. When we come to the part where it is suggested that we let come to mind those family and friends to whom we would like to wish well-being, this time try listening to our heart. Let it inform us of what it might be that our friend really needs, rather than using our knowledge of them to reason what that might be. (You may have been doing this already, in which case just continue.)

MAIN AIM OF THIS MEETING

The aim of this session is to explore further a model of how meditation works.

This will form a basis for an understanding of why certain aspects of practice are important for the development and application of meditation.

PRACTICAL POINTS FOR RUNNING THE MEETING

THE MEDITATION

The coordinator will have to initiate the meditation and remind the group about the change of emphasis in today's meditation (see sample text). This time everyone should consider doing the relaxation part of the meditation by themselves.

THE CONSULTATION

The object of this session is to explore how meditation can help us feel more inspired and uplifted and what gets in the way of this happening. It is not necessary to get into deliberations about whether certain activities are good or bad but just stick to what consequences they have for our state of consciousness.

HELLO TIME

Coordinator

Allow an appropriate period of time for people to say hello and chat.

Focus the group.

Ask how everyone has got on since the last meeting.

Invite sharing of contributions of any writings, poetry, thoughts that may have been brought relating to the last meeting.

Remind group of today's focus, if necessary, e.g.

Today we are going to look at the basic principles of how meditation works.

This will give us an understanding of why certain aspects of practice are important and help us to develop our ability to meditate and bring its benefits into our lives.

Enquire how everyone feels about doing the relaxation part of the meditation by themselves. (Encourage this but go with the wishes of anyone who might find this difficult.)

SETTLING DOWN

Coordinator

Remind the group:

During the meditation period this time, to help us listen to our intuition and know ourselves better, we will practise what could be called 'listening with the heart'. At the part where it is

34

suggested that we let a friend come to mind to whom we'd like to wish well-being, this time try listening to our heart. Let it inform us of what it might be that our friend really needs, rather than using our knowledge of them to reason what that might be.

As last time, that part of the meditation will be followed by about five minutes' silence, towards the end of which there will be a short reading.

Any questions/comments?

Switch off/unplug phones, use the toilet, etc. Settle into silence with some music.

MEDITATION PERIOD

MEDITATION

Coordinator

Begin the meditation by reading this. (For the simplified CALM course play CD from track 6. Remember to read out the passage indicated below towards the end of the silent period.)

Sitting comfortably and upright, with our eyes closed, breathing naturally, let's begin.

Just as we begin now it's always useful to be awake to the present moment and remind ourselves that we are doing this practice because there are wonderful benefits to be had – for the way we feel, for our mental abilities, for our body, our life in general.

And as we begin now, let's turn our attention inwards, towards our hearts, and see if we can get a feeling of what it might be that we need from the meditation today – perhaps peace, love, healing, confirmation, understanding, courage – whatever feels right for us today.

Whether we've found something specific or have a vague longing, let's commit ourselves now to spending the rest of this short period of time today for the nurturing of our souls.

For this short while, we let go of all our agendas, our responsibilities, our worries and concerns; forget everything else for now and allow ourselves to go into this meditation which will benefit all aspects of our lives anyway.

We start by focusing our attention within our bodies, with our feet resting firmly on the ground.

And then, by ourselves, just check through and make sure all parts of our bodies are comfortable and relaxed.

Allow a couple of minutes for everyone to do their relaxation.

Then use the recorded meditation starting with the breathing exercise on track 8: *'Now with our bodies comfortable and relaxed, we move on to focusing our attention on the sensations of breathing.'*

Towards the end of the period of silence which follows the meditation read this passage:

Consider how a pure, well-polished mirror fully reflects the effulgence of the sun, no matter how distant the sun may be. As soon as the mirror is cleaned and purified, the sun will manifest itself. The more pure and sanctified the heart of man becomes, the nearer it draws to God, and the light of the Sun of Reality is revealed within it. This light sets hearts aglow with the fire of the love of God, opens in them the doors of knowledge and unseals the divine mysteries so that spiritual discoveries are made possible.

'Abdu'l-Bahá[7]

Allow a short while for reflection, then bring the meditation period to a close:

Could we all bring our attention back into the room now and focus our attention on our feet resting firmly on the ground. (Give people a minute to readjust.)

CONSULTATION
FEEDBACK

Coordinator

Invite feedback from meditation.

Possible Questions

- Is there anything about the meditation you'd like to share with us?

- How did you get on with 'listening with the heart'?

TODAY'S FOCUS – PRINCIPLES OF MEDITATION

Coordinator

Introduce today's focus and initiate consultation.

Read and discuss the quotations in a manner that suits the group.

Quotations

Consider how a pure, well-polished mirror fully reflects the effulgence of the sun, no matter how distant the sun may be. As soon as the mirror is cleaned and purified, the sun will manifest itself. The more pure and sanctified the heart of man becomes, the nearer it draws to God, and the light of the Sun of Reality is revealed within it. This light sets hearts aglow with the fire of the love of God, opens in them the doors of knowledge and unseals the divine mysteries so that spiritual discoveries are made possible.[8]

Upon the inmost reality of each and every created thing He hath shed the light of one of His names, and made it a recipient of the glory of one of His attributes. Upon the reality of man, however, He hath focused the radiance of all of His names and attributes, and made it a mirror of His own Self . . .

These energies with which the Day Star of Divine bounty . . . hath endowed the reality of man lie, however, latent within him . . . The radiance of these energies may be obscured by worldly desires even as the light of the sun can be concealed beneath the dust and dross which cover the mirror.[9]

36

Definition

Latent: Hidden, concealed; present but not manifest, exhibited or developed.[10]

Possible Questions

Quotation 1

- In this passage what do the sun and mirror represent?
- If we wanted to reflect the sun with a mirror what would we have to do with it?
- What does the passage suggest needs to happen if the mirror is to reflect the sun more fully?
- What occurs when the mirror of our heart is cleansed?
- What could be some of the effects we feel when this spiritual light shines on us?

Quotation 2

- What could being a mirror of God mean?
- What are some examples of these spiritual attributes?
- What causes the dust that covers the mirror and obscures its radiance?
- What could be some examples of this dust of worldly desires?
- Is there anything wrong with trying to live physical life fully?
- What can we do about the dust on our 'mirrors'?

SUMMARY
Coordinator

Summarize if necessary.

CONCLUDE
Coordinator

Anything else to share?

SOCIALIZE

In meeting 3 we looked at how our hearts are like mirrors that can potentially receive and reflect God's love, knowledge and other qualities.

The sun (God, our higher self) and the mirror (our soul, our consciousness) are always there, but 'dust' obstructs the sun's rays, limiting our potential to receive and reflect light.

Dust could be any worldly thoughts or feelings that fill our consciousness and have the effect of leaving less room, or no room, for higher consciousness.

One perspective of what 'worldly desires' implies could be this. Desire is a natural expression of the spirit of life within us, seeking to live and express itself. Our feeling of desire can be directed out towards things of the world or be turned in towards spiritual things – finding the balance is the challenge.

If our focus on natural worldly needs is carried to excess it can become an obstacle to meeting our needs as a whole. The need to eat, for example, if carried to excess, can lead to obesity, which limits our ability to do other things.

The more our thoughts and striving are focused on meeting our physical needs, the less room there is left in our consciousness for anything else. Through habit, these thoughts, feelings, hopes, fears, anxieties, etc. keep coming into our consciousness and when we are endeavouring to meditate they make it difficult for us to tune into our inner world and be nourished from it. From this perspective the obscuring dust on our mirror is the outcome of worldly desires.

In relation to our practice of meditation, 'dust' could be seen in two ways. One is the immediate dust: the thoughts and feelings that are the consequences of whatever is happening for us today – an argument we've had, some good or bad news. The various meditation exercises, and the skills we acquire from them, can help us to calm things down and clear our consciousness.

The other is the more established dust: the ways of thinking and feeling that have become a habit for us, like having an anxious, over-active mind or a defeatist or arrogant attitude. It is the regular effective practice that will, layer by layer, polish this dust away. The more we practise polishing our 'mirror' with mindful, liberating, life-enhancing attitudes the more they become part of us and the easier it is for us to receive and reflect the light.

When we sit to meditate:

- we are turning away from the material world to the spiritual sun
- we are performing meditation exercises that are polishing our mirror

and when we are practising regularly

- we are preventing dust resettling, polishing more stubborn dust and perfecting the finish of the mirror

For all of our sakes let's choose to polish our mirrors more regularly.

4

Focusing

Learning to focus our attention will help us both enter the meditative state and remain in it – and the longer we can remain in a state of meditation the more benefit and insight we will get from it. Generally, however, the ability to concentrate our attention in one direction is underdeveloped, so after a few seconds of trying, sounds, thoughts or emotions distract us. The breathing exercise that we use is of great value in this regard.

There are many variations of breathing exercises to be found and during the CALM course everyone should feel free to improvise and do what feels most suitable to them. In this next meeting we are going to use a variation of the breathing exercise we have used so far, which some people find a bit easier.

This is what will happen. First we will go through the relaxation by ourselves again, like last time. Then whoever is coordinating will remind us of the simple points we need to follow (see below) and we will practise the new breathing exercise by ourselves.

The new breathing exercise is very similar to the breathing exercise that we already do:

- breath in and out experiencing the sensations of breathing
- experience the breath where it suits you: abdomen, heart level, etc.

but in addition

- after each out breath, count the breath (breath in and out, count one to yourself; breath in and out, count two to yourself; etc. up to the 9th breath, then start again)
- give 90 per cent of your attention to experiencing the breath and 10 per cent to counting
- improvise to suit yourself if necessary

MAIN AIMS OF THIS MEETING

To understand the value of learning to keep our attention focused, both to help us enter a state of meditation and to use it more effectively.

To look at the value of the use of the breathing exercise.

PRACTICAL POINTS FOR RUNNING THE MEETING

The Meditation

Everyone will be practising the relaxation by themselves. Following this the coordinator will use the simple instructions provided to lead the breathing exercise. It would help if whoever is to be the coordinator practised both the exercise itself and reading the text a day or so beforehand.

The CD will be started from track 9, at what is referred to as the attunement – 'Now we return our attention to the level of the heart . . . but this time, just as with each breath we allow in the air that keeps our bodies alive, this time, with each breath, we open our hearts to let in the love that our soul needs to feel alive.'

HELLO TIME

Coordinator

Allow an appropriate period of time for people to say hello and chat.

Focus the group.

Ask everyone how they have got on since the last meeting.

Invite sharing of contributions of any writings, poetry, thoughts that may have been brought, relating to the last meeting.

Remind the group of today's focus, if necessary, e.g.

To understand the value of being able to keep our attention focused, both to help us enter a state of meditation and to use it more effectively.

Look at the value of the breathing exercise.

SETTLING DOWN

Coordinator

Remind everyone about doing the relaxation part of the meditation by themselves.

Enquire whether everyone understands today's breathing exercise.

Explain, if necessary, as in part 1 of this section.

Settle down in silence with some music.

MEDITATION PERIOD
MEDITATION

Coordinator

Begin the meditation by reading this. (For the simplified CALM course play CD from track 6.)

Sitting comfortably and upright, with our eyes closed, breathing naturally, let's begin.

Just as we begin now, it's always useful to be awake to the present moment and remind ourselves that we are doing this practice because there are wonderful benefits to be had – for the way we feel, for our mental abilities, for our body, our life in general.

And now let's listen to our hearts for a moment to get a feeling of what is it that we might need from the meditation today – perhaps peace, love, healing, understanding, courage – whatever feels right for us today.

Whether we've found something specific or just a vague longing, let's commit ourselves now to spending this short period of time today to the nurturing of our souls.

For this short while we let go all our agendas, our responsibilities, our worries and concerns; forget everything else for now and allow ourselves to go into this meditation which will benefit all aspects of our lives.

We start by focusing our attention within our bodies, with our feet resting firmly on the ground.

And then by ourselves just check through and make sure all parts of our bodies are comfortable and relaxed.

Allow a couple of minutes for everyone to do their relaxation.

Then begin the breathing exercise by reading the following:

Now with our bodies relaxed we move on to focusing our attention on the sensations of breathing.

Feel free to focus your attention wherever it suits you.

With each breath we experience the feelings of expansion and relaxation.

With each breath we allow our attention to become absorbed in these sensations.

but in addition:

after each out breath, we count the breath.

Breath in . . . and out, count one to yourself; breath in . . . and out, count two to yourself . . . up to the ninth breath, then start again.

Give 90 per cent of your attention to experiencing the breath and 10 per cent to counting

Improvise to suit yourself if necessary.

After a couple of minutes remind everyone:

And remember, when at any time we are distracted by things around us, or thoughts from within, whatever they are, once we become aware of them, never let ourselves become frustrated at having lost our focus; make everything part of the meditation. Just notice whatever it is attentively for a few seconds and then return to . . . focusing our attention on the sensations of breathing and counting the breaths.

Give everyone five minutes to practise their breathing exercise then indicate that it's time to move on to following the recorded meditation.

Start the CD from track 9: 'Now we return our attention to the level of the heart.'

Towards the end of the period of silence which follows the meditation read this passage:

So long as the thoughts of an individual are scattered he will achieve no results, but if his thinking be concentrated on a single point wonderful will be the fruits thereof.
. . . once the sun shineth upon a concave mirror, or on a lens that is convex, all its heat will be concentrated on a single point, and that one point will burn the hottest. Thus is it necessary to focus one's thinking on a single point so that it will become an effective force.[11]

Allow a short while for reflection, then bring the meditation period to a close:

Could we all bring our attention back into the room now and focus our attention on our feet resting firmly on the ground. (Give people a minute to readjust.)

CONSULTATION
TODAY'S FOCUS – FOCUSING

Coordinator

Introduce today's focus and initiate sharing of feedback and consultation.

Today's focus is about the importance of learning to keep our attention focused so that we are able to reach a state of meditation and also get more benefit from it.

Invite feedback from meditation.

Possible Questions

Today's quotation proposed that it is necessary to focus our thinking to make it an effective force.

- How did you find your concentration was with this new breathing exercise?
- Did you prefer the one we used before?
- Did anybody improvise and do it their own way?
- Do you think it would be helpful for you to improve your concentration?

- Do you think the use of a breathing exercise could help improve concentration?
- Are there any other ways you can think of?
- Any other thoughts about the quotation? (Perhaps read it again.)

Quotation

Read quotation and discuss.

The following quotation suggests some of the benefits of being able to remain more focused.

> *The meditative faculty is akin to the mirror; if you put it before earthly objects it will reflect them. Therefore if the spirit of man is contemplating earthly subjects he will be informed of these.*
> *But if you turn the mirror of your spirits heavenwards, the heavenly constellations and the rays of the Sun of Reality will be reflected in your hearts, and the virtues of the Kingdom will be obtained.*[12]

Possible Questions

- What are the implications of reflecting, i.e. being like a mirror?
- How can we learn to become more receptive?
- What are examples of some of the 'earthly' things about which we could get understanding?
- What are some examples of the benefits of being able to focus in a spiritual direction, i.e. turn the mirror of our spirits heavenwards?

Definition

Contemplate: from Latin: *con* – with; *templum* – open space for observation

SUMMARY
Coordinator

Some possible points to identify/underline in summary:

- We need to learn to focus our attention more effectively.
- We need to be able to maintain our focus – sit and reflect without losing it.
- Once we are focused, towards whatever we direct our attention we will become informed.
- The more we practise the easier it will become.

CONCLUDE
Coordinator

Anything else to share?

SOCIALIZE

This time we looked at the importance of being able to keep our attention focused if we are to be able to reach a state of meditation and also get more benefit from it. We also looked at the usefulness of the breathing exercise in developing concentration.

As well as developing mindfulness and concentration this sort of practice provides newcomers to meditation with something tangible to work with. It also exercises our capacity to make choices in our inner world – to choose what we are experiencing – and by focusing our attention on the sensations of breathing, our consciousness is opened to tuning into, and being with, the experience of the inner world. As it has the effect of settling thoughts and emotions it makes our consciousness more receptive for the next stage of the meditation as well.

Another thing that happens is that we begin to associate feelings of peacefulness with breathing and that can be very helpful conditioning when things get stressful – take a deep breath, tune in, be detached, just observe before we react.

Fitting in more meditation practice into a very busy life may become stressful itself but there must be some times throughout the day when we could fit in a few calming breaths. Perhaps we could all look for a few of these spaces and let everyone know how we got on next time.

5

Attunement

The topic in the last meeting was about using the repetitive mental act of focusing on our breathing to help develop our concentration and prepare our consciousness for entering the state of meditation. This session is about exploring the use of repetitive heartfelt invocation as a means of attuning ourselves to the spirit within, to that deeper level of consciousness – entering the state of meditation.

This type of meditation exercise is practised in all the major spiritual traditions and uses what is commonly known in Hinduism and Buddhism as a mantra – a word or phrase with particular relevance that is repeated inwardly or chanted. In Sufism, the mystic branch of Islam, this type of practice was called *dhikr* and a Sufi would repeat a phrase, perhaps from the Qur'án, with the intention of achieving spiritual union with his Beloved – God. Returning to the analogy of the sun and the mirror, *dhikr* is polishing the mirror. This is the same form of devotional activity that a Bahá'í would perform with the daily repetition of Alláh-u-Abhá (God is All-Glorious).

In English *dhikr* translates as 'remembrance' but it means more than remembering, as will be emphasized in this session's quotation. When reading today's quotation perhaps we could bear in mind that a specific form of meditation is one of the meanings of the term 'remembrance'.

In this coming meeting's meditation we are going to allow ourselves to be open to being inspired with a word or phrase, the repetition of which will act as a focus for tuning into whatever comfort or strength we may need – in other words, we will make our own 'mantra'. This is how it will go.

The meditation period will start in the usual way, with just a little guidance by whoever is coordinating to keep us all together. Then when we reach the stage where we normally focus in our hearts and open them to goodness, we will try working with the following guidance which we will be reminded of at the time.

- Focus our attention in our hearts.
- Tune in to what our heart feels it needs right now.
- Listen for a word or phrase that sums up our heart's desire (go in peace, come alive, be with love, one with all, God loves me, etc.; or just use one word – healing, strength).
- Whatever it is, it has to be right for us personally.

Perhaps our backgrounds have phrases that would be suitable and easy to repeat: 'Is there any remover of difficulties save God?'; 'Be still and know that I am God'; 'I honour the divine within'; etc.

As we repeat this word or phrase, allow most of our attention to be with the feeling and just a little bit to be with the words – the words just act as an anchor that helps our mind and heart remain focused.

For this type of meditation to work we are trying to encourage the energy behind our desire for peace, or for whatever we are aspiring, to be greater than the energy behind other desires we may have, otherwise they will tend to surface into our consciousness and hamper our efforts at meditation.

This is an extension of the affirmation we practise at the beginning of each meditation – finding a heartfelt reason for why we are meditating – but in this case finding a word or phrase that sums up our affirmation and repeating it, as with a mantra.

MAIN AIM OF THIS MEETING

To explore the use of repetitive heartfelt invocation (focusing with the heart) as a means of attuning ourselves to the Spirit/deeper level of consciousness within.

PRACTICAL POINTS FOR RUNNING THE MEETING

Everyone will be practising the relaxation and breathing exercise by themselves with a little bit of guidance just to keep us all together. It would help if whoever is to be coordinator both practised the exercise and read the text themselves a day or so beforehand.

HELLO TIME

Coordinator

Allow an appropriate period of time for people to say hello and chat.

Focus the group.

Ask how everyone has got on since the last meeting.

Did anyone manage to fit a few calming breaths into the daily routine?

SETTLING DOWN

Coordinator

Remind everyone about doing the relaxation and breathing part of the meditation by themselves.

Enquire whether everyone understands today's meditation.

Settle down in silence with some music.

MEDITATION PERIOD
MEDITATION

Coordinator

Begin the meditation by reading this. (For the simplified CALM course play CD from track 6.)

Sitting comfortably and upright, with our eyes closed, breathing naturally, let's begin.

Just as we begin now, it's always useful to be awake to the present moment and remind ourselves that we are doing this practice because there are wonderful benefits to be had – for the way we feel, for our mental abilities, for our body, our life in general.

And now let's listen to our hearts for a moment to get a feeling of what it is that we might need from the meditation today – perhaps peace, love, healing, understanding, courage – whatever feels right for us today.

Whether we've found something specific or just a vague longing, let's commit ourselves now to spending this short period of time today to the nurturing of our souls.

For this short while we let go all our agendas, our responsibilities, our worries and concerns; forget everything else for now and allow ourselves to go into this meditation which will benefit all aspects of our lives.

We start by focusing our attention within our bodies, with our feet resting firmly on the ground.

And then by ourselves just check through and make sure all parts of our bodies are comfortable and relaxed.

Allow a couple of minutes for everyone to go through their relaxation.

Then begin the breathing exercise by reading the following:

Now with our bodies relaxed we move on to focusing our attention on the sensations of breathing.

Feel free to focus your attention wherever it suits you.

With each breath we experience the feelings of expansion and relaxation.

With each breath we allow our attention to become absorbed in these sensations.

After a couple of minutes remind everyone:

And remember, when at any time we are distracted by things around us, or thoughts from within, whatever they are, once we become aware of them, never let ourselves become frustrated at having lost our focus; make everything part of the meditation. Just notice whatever it is attentively for a few seconds and then return to . . . focusing our attention on the sensations of breathing.

Give everyone a few minutes to practise their breathing exercise then indicate that it's time to move on:

Now we return our attention to the level of the heart.

Focus our attention in our hearts . . . tune in to what your heart feels it needs right now . . . how it wants to be.

Listen for a word or phrase that sums up your heart's desire.

Whatever it is, it has to be just right for us personally.

If nothing comes just stay with your heart and ask it compassionately how it would like to feel.

As we repeat this word or phrase, allow most of our attention to be with the feeling and just a little bit to be with the words – the words just act as an anchor that helps our mind and heart remain focused.

If we find it appropriate, the word or phrase could change as the meditation progresses.

After what feels like an appropriate period of time – five minutes or more – invite the group to spend a few minutes in silence.

Towards the end of the period of silence read this passage:

> . . . give thy best attention to the remembrance of God, that thy heart may at all times be animated with His Spirit, and not be shut out as by a veil from thy Best Beloved. Let not thy tongue pay lip service in praise of God while thy heart be not attuned to the exalted Summit of Glory, and the Focal Point of communion.'[13]

Allow a short while for reflection, then bring the meditation period to a close:

> Could we all bring our attention back into the room now and focus our attention on our feet resting firmly on the ground. (Give people a minute to readjust.)

CONSULTATION
TODAY'S FOCUS – ATTUNEMENT

Coordinator

Introduce today's focus and initiate sharing of feedback and consultation.

> In today's focus we are exploring the use of repetitive heartfelt invocation (focusing with the heart) as a means of attuning ourselves to the Spirit within/deeper level of consciousness.

Invite feedback from meditation.

Possible Questions

- How did you manage with finding your own invocation, your mantra?
- Would anyone like to share what came to them?
- Does anyone normally use this type of meditation and how do you get on with it?

Recalling that the term 'remembrance' in one sense refers to the mantric type of meditation we have been practising today:

- What does the first sentence indicate will be an outcome of giving this form of meditation our 'best attention'?
- What does the second sentence of the quotation tell us about this? (Perhaps read the quotation again.)

Quotation

> . . . give thy best attention to the remembrance of God, that thy heart may at all times be animated with His Spirit, and not be shut out as by a veil from thy Best Beloved. Let not thy

tongue pay lip service in praise of God while thy heart be not attuned to the exalted Summit of Glory, and the Focal Point of communion.[14]

Definitions

Mantra: In Hinduism and Buddhism, a holy name or word, for inward meditation; a repeated phrase, sentence or refrain used as a prayer or incantation

Attunement: Bring into harmony or accord; make perfectly suited or receptive to[15]

CONCLUDE

Coordinator

> Anything else to share?
>
> Summarize if necessary.

SOCIALIZE

CULTIVATING HUMILITY AND PATIENCE

If we think back to the analogy of the sun and the mirror it is obvious that though the mirror reflects the light it is not the source of the light. In the same way, we reflect love and other spiritual qualities into the world – we can see ourselves as an expression of the universe, not the source of it.

Let's imagine that, after the darkness and cold of winter, spring has now arrived and it is a beautiful day. We decide to leave the house to sit outside and enjoy the sunshine. Though the sky is blue, there are several fluffy white clouds obscuring the sun but we sit anyway because we know that the clouds will pass and soon the warm invigorating sun will shine upon us.

In the same way, in meditation we should know the inner sun will shine but we cannot force it, any more than we have the power to hurry away the clouds in the sky. We sit there, being still, using our invocation/mantra to remain receptive – and wait.

When we feel the sun break through the clouds and its golden rays fall upon us, we open like flowers to them and fall in love with their warmth. The more we become attuned to that source of love we feel within us, the more we become embraced and enraptured by it; and the more we will yearn to let it radiate out into all areas of our lives.

Employing the sun and mirror analogy again, during the first part of any period of meditation that uses an invocation/mantra, our heart, endeavouring to attune itself, may be more receptive in nature – like the mirror longing for the light. Later in the meditation when we become more attuned, the feeling in our heart may be more expressive, like the mirror reflecting the light it has received. So part way through a meditation we may change the invocation/mantra we use or perhaps just change the emphasis in the words we are using.

Tuning in with our heart is a way of getting close to our true and inmost self. When we put time aside to practise it we get to know and understand ourselves better but it is also something that we can do at any quiet time – when we awake or are going to sleep or when waiting for a bus. We can be sitting in the sun wherever we are. Why not try it 'at all times', as it says in the quotation?

6

Developing Our Practice

The underlying aim of the CALM course so far has been to create the conditions and provide the information that would help us understand and experience meditation – to connect with our inner essence, with God or however we would describe it.

In the coming meetings we will be looking towards practising meditation more effectively and bringing its benefits into our lives.

In the last meeting, during the silent part of meditation, we allowed ourselves to become open to a word or phrase that was meaningful to us. This session will be about learning to be open to receiving inspiration and understanding in a more focused way during the silent period of our meditation.

To give us something to work with we're going to look at developing or improving our own regular practice of meditation.

This is how it will work. We will start with a shorter version of our normal meditation – the relaxation, breathing exercise and attunement – with just a little bit of instruction from the coordinator. Then just after the beginning of the silent period that follows the coordinator will ask some questions.

For those of us who are not practising regularly but want to try to do so, the meditation will be specifically aimed at putting together regular daily practice. For those of us who do meditate regularly we can review our practice with a view to making it more effective.

MAIN AIMS OF THIS MEETING

To explore the use of meditation for dealing with particular issues.

Today, that is either to develop or to improve our own regular practice.

PRACTICAL POINTS FOR RUNNING THE MEETING

Everyone will be practising the relaxation and breathing exercise by themselves with a little bit of guidance just to keep us all together. It would help if whoever is to be coordinator both practised the exercise and read the text themselves a day or so beforehand.

HELLO TIME

Coordinator

Allow an appropriate period of time for people to say hello and chat.

Focus the group.

Did anyone manage to work with listening to their hearts or using their own mantra?

SETTLING DOWN

Coordinator

Remind everyone about doing the relaxation and breathing part of the meditation by themselves.

Enquire whether everyone is clear about today's meditation, as in part 1 of this section.

Settle down in silence with some music.

MEDITATION PERIOD

MEDITATION

Coordinator

Begin the meditation by reading this passage. (For the simplified CALM course play CD from track 6. Also, after a shortened silent period, read the passage starting, 'Now as we sit here . . .' and invite feedback about this exercise during consultation.)

Sitting comfortably and upright, with our eyes closed, breathing naturally, let's begin.

Just as we begin now it's always useful to be awake to the present moment and remind ourselves why we are doing this practice and commit ourselves to spending this short period of time today for the nurturing of our souls.

Next we focus our attention within our bodies with our feet resting firmly on the ground.

And then, by ourselves, just check through and make sure all parts of our bodies are comfortable and relaxed.

Allow a couple of minutes for everyone to go through their relaxation.

Then begin the breathing exercise by reading the following:

> Now with our bodies relaxed we move on to focusing our attention on the sensations of breathing.
>
> Feel free to focus your attention wherever it suits you.
>
> With each breath we experience the feelings of expansion and relaxation.
>
> With each breath we allow our attention to become absorbed in these sensations.

After a couple of minutes remind everyone:

> And remember, when at any time we are distracted by things around us, or thoughts from within, whatever they are, once we become aware of them, never let ourselves become frustrated at having lost our focus; make everything part of the meditation. Just notice whatever it is attentively for a few seconds and then return to . . . focusing our attention on the sensations of breathing.

Give everyone a few minutes to practise their breathing exercise then indicate that it's time to move on:

> Now we turn our attention to the level of our heart . . . and once again, with each breath in, we open our hearts to be filled with loving kindliness, or peacefulness or whatever we need.

(Pause for a minute.)

> Now as we sit here, let's think of the place where it would feel best for us to meditate – preferably, for convenience, somewhere at home but it could be somewhere else nearby.
>
> Is there anything we need to do first before we meditate? Tell someone, unplug the phone?
>
> Imagine ourselves being there. What time of day it is. What time would be best for us.
>
> Is there anything we would like to do to make this place special? Flowers, fragrance, light, comfort, warmth?
>
> Take a few minutes and just imagine yourself in your special spot. How would you like to feel . . . physically . . . mentally . . . emotionally.

(Pause for a few minutes.)

> Would it feel OK to allow yourself space to be here in your sacred spot regularly? How about choosing to commit yourself to doing this? Something that will be better for you . . . and those around you.
>
> If it feels OK, resolve to do it.
>
> > Now let's spend a few minutes of personal space in silence.

Allow an appropriate period for reflection, then bring the meditation to a close:

Could we all bring our attention back into the room now and focus our attention on our feet resting firmly on the ground. (Give people a minute to readjust.)

CONSULTATION
FEEDBACK

Coordinator

Go around the group and invite feedback.

Possible questions:

Would anybody like to share how they got on with the meditation?

How did you feel about committing yourself to regular practice?

CONCLUDE
Coordinator

Anything else to share?

SOCIALIZE

Changing the routine of our lives is a challenge but if we know meditation is important for us we owe it to ourselves to keep trying. There will be times when we do not keep up our practice but when we feel the need to start again, just begin again and again – just as when we get distracted in the breathing exercise – without getting frustrated with ourselves.

7

Releasing Potential

In this session we will look at how it is that although we all have such wonderful potential as human beings, some of the habitual patterns of thinking and feeling we have acquired can imprison this spiritual capacity within us.

Whatever we practise, whatever we do regularly, we get good at – whether it is helpful or harmful to us. To be liberated from our limiting patterns we need to regularly draw upon the spiritual resources within us all and be refreshed by them.

Through the regular practice of meditation we will be more able to release our potential as human beings and live more fulfilled lives. However, although we need to practise regularly, our attitude towards spiritual growth should be a compassionate, nurturing one, not a forceful process.

MAIN AIMS OF THIS MEETING

To identify the vital role of regular, nurturing practice in freeing us from ingrained limitations.

To identify the need to draw upon our spiritual resources to help us.

PRACTICAL POINTS FOR RUNNING THE MEETING

The meditation is to be heart-centred and could be the same as the ones we used earlier in the CALM course, with the coordinator providing a little bit of guidance, using the sample text or CD.

Use the quotation provided during the silent period as it is relevant for today.

Alternatively, the group could decide how it would prefer the meditation to be.

HELLO TIME

Coordinator

> After there has been time to say hello and chat, focus the group.
>
> Ask how everyone has got on since the last meeting.
>
>> Would anybody like to share how they have been getting on since last time?
>
> Discuss how the group would prefer to have the meditation run today but preferably keep the meditation heart-centred.

SETTLING DOWN

Settle down with some music.

MEDITATION PERIOD

MEDITATION

Coordinator

> Begin the meditation as chosen by the group.
>
> If using the example below, for the 'attunement' part, make up your own, use the sample text or use the recording as preferred. (For the simplified CALM course play CD from track 6.)
>
>> Sitting comfortably and upright, with our eyes closed, breathing naturally, let's begin.
>>
>> Just as we begin now it's always useful to be awake to the present moment and remind ourselves why we are doing this practice and commit ourselves to spending this short period of time today for the nurturing of our souls.
>>
>> Next we focus our attention within our bodies with our feet resting firmly on the ground.

And then, by ourselves, just check through and make sure all parts of our bodies are comfortable and relaxed.

Allow a couple of minutes for everyone to go through their relaxation.

Then begin the breathing exercise by reading the following:

Now with our bodies relaxed we move on to focusing our attention on the sensations of breathing.

Feel free to focus your attention wherever it suits you.

With each breath we experience the feelings of expansion and relaxation.

With each breath we allow our attention to become absorbed in these sensations.

After a couple of minutes remind everyone:

And remember, when at any time we are distracted by things around us, or thoughts from within, whatever they are, once we become aware of them, never let ourselves become frustrated at having lost our focus; make everything part of the meditation. Just notice whatever it is attentively for a few seconds and then return to . . . focusing our attention on the sensations of breathing.

Give everyone a few minutes to practise their breathing exercise then indicate that it's time to move on:

(Attunement)

Now we return our attention to the level of the heart.

But this time, just as with each breath we allow in the air that keeps our bodies alive, this time, with each breath, we open our hearts to let in the love that our soul needs to feel alive.

With each breath in we open our hearts to let in love or peace or healing or whatever is needed.

With each breath we open our hearts like flowers opening their petals to the sun, from which they receive their light and life . . . Without striving, we too open our hearts to let in the spiritual sunlight.

The more we love the light, the warmer we feel its glow; the more we fall in love with love itself, the stronger it grows within us.
We let ourselves feel grateful for and cherish the spirit that brings life and fills our hearts.

And as we continue to open our hearts, with each breath, to be filled with the light of love, we also now remember others who are in need.

Beginning with those close to us, we allow a wish to arise in our hearts that they too may have more of the peace or love or healing or whatever they need in their lives.

We let love into our hearts and we let it out towards them.

Then let someone who we don't know come to mind – someone we saw in a shop or in the street recently – and in the same way let in goodness and let it out towards them also.

Now as we continue to open our hearts, as we need to, we let our consciousness expand to include others in the world.

Gradually, we expand our thoughts and wishes of well-being to include wider circles of people; beginning with our meditation group, dear souls all of us – each in need of something more in our lives. We let love into our hearts and we let it out.

Then move on, in our own time, to larger groups or communities, until we include all of the peoples of the world. We let in love and let out wishes of peace and well-being and unity.

And now, before we go into a period of silence for personal reflection, we feel appreciation for that Great Universal Source from which all life and comfort and strength comes.

We can now spend a few minutes in silence for personal reflection.

Towards the end of the silent period after whichever meditation has been used, read this passage:

Man is the supreme Talisman. Lack of a proper education hath, however, deprived him of that which he doth inherently possess . . . Regard man as a mine rich in gems of inestimable value. Education can, alone, cause it to reveal its treasures, and enable mankind to benefit therefrom.[16]

Allow a period for reflection then bring the meditation to a close:

Could we all bring our attention back into the room now and focus our attention on our feet resting firmly on the ground. (Give people a minute to readjust.)

CONSULTATION
FEEDBACK

Coordinator

Invite feedback about the meditation.

Move on to study the quotations, as appropriate.

Quotations

Man is the supreme Talisman. Lack of a proper education hath, however, deprived him of that which he doth inherently possess . . . Regard man as a mine rich in gems of inestimable value. Education can, alone, cause it to reveal its treasures, and enable mankind to benefit therefrom.[17]

Man is always apt to fall into the habit of doing a thing in a certain way, and thereby become captive to prescribed forms.[18]

68

The only power that is capable of delivering man from this captivity is the power of the breaths of the Holy Spirit.[19]

Through the faculty of meditation man . . . receives the breath of the Holy Spirit – the bestowal of the Spirit is given in reflection and meditation.[20]

Possible Questions

Quotation 1

- What could being like 'a mine rich in gems' mean?
- Can anyone think of examples of how our education or upbringing can limit our potential to release these qualities?

Quotation 2

- Why are we apt to become captive to particular habits?
- What are some examples of habits we adopt that are not helpful either to ourselves or to others?

Quotation 3

- What can free us from captivity?
- What does this mean – how do we experience the help of the 'Holy Spirit'?
- Why might it be the only power that can deliver us?

Quotation 4

- What is one way we can receive the help of the 'Holy Spirit'?

CONCLUDE

Coordinator

Summarize if necessary.

Anything else to share?

SOCIALIZE

Although we all have such wonderful potential as human beings, acquired habitual patterns of thinking, feeling and behaving imprison this spiritual capacity within us. Whatever we practise, whatever we do regularly, we get good at – whether it is helpful or harmful to us. In meditation we are able to receive the spiritual help we need to be liberated from our unhelpful patterns of thinking, feeling and responding. If we practise meditation regularly and effectively it will have an effect.

In the physical world around us we all have amazing capacities. Just going shopping is an activity that requires many physical and mental skills, which as babies we did not possess but have since acquired. One reason we can manage the world around us is because we have learned to identify objects and understand what they do. We see and identify an object, which is named a kettle, and we know that it will contain and heat another object named water, and with this, and other such knowledge and ingredients, we have the power to make a cup of tea.

When it comes to our inner world we are not taught to recognize and understand what it is made of and how it works, so is it surprising that we can end up in a mess? Who would, after putting on a blindfold, try to make a cake in a strange kitchen? And yet this is what we try to do with our spiritual and emotional lives.

Meditations similar to the following one have been regularly practised for thousands of years to help people cultivate mindfulness and begin the process of understanding their inner lives. They recognized that simply giving thoughts or feelings a name was the first step in learning to manage them. Try playing with this exercise for a short while during the coming week.

- Start your meditation as normal, e.g. with a short relaxation.

- Then using any simple breathing exercise to keep you focused, just become an observer of whatever enters your consciousness.

- Whatever comes – thought, feeling or sensation – identify it and let it have a name: e.g. contentment, too hot, confused, memory, idea, car passing, daydream, irritated, peaceful.

- Repeat the name to yourself inwardly for a short while but allow most of your consciousness to be an interested observer of the experience of whatever it is you have named. The name is just like an anchor that keep us in place.

- Then move back to the breathing exercise or on to the next naming and repeat the process as long as it feels useful.

8

Nurturing Change

This time we are going to look at something that in a very subtle way can sabotage our efforts to meditate regularly – resistance to practice. This is something we need to be aware of and manage effectively for our efforts with meditation to progress.

Part of us wants to change, to become whatever it is we are meant to be, but also there is the part that doesn't – for it has spent years developing strategies for protecting itself against hurt and promoting what at the time were perceived to be our best interests.

When that part of us that wants to grow is sufficiently motivated to take the initiative and, for instance, chooses to learn to meditate, then it is inevitable that there will be resistance from the other well-established part of us that will feel its security being threatened.

This inner resistance to change manifests itself in many disguises as resistance to meditation and is something we have to be aware of and deal with as part of our regular practice. However, having a battle with that part of ourselves which is concerned with stability and security is not a useful or effective way of moving forward.

When, in meditation, we find the inner sanctuary of our true self and experience the genuine security of this loving, creative source of life, then all parts of our self are content to merge into this centre and from this point we can be inspired to move forward in unity.

The attitude towards regular practice, our spiritual growth, should be one of compassion, not forcefulness. Seeds do not instantly become flowers – a healthy nurturing process of growth is needed. If we practise learning to listen to our inner world we will develop our capacity to receive the insights and inspiration from the 'Divine Spirit' of which 'Abdu'l-Bahá spoke and which, in turn, will empower us to transform.

MAIN AIMS OF THIS MEETING

To look at resistance to meditation.

To underline how our spiritual practice should be a nurturing process, not a battle zone.

PRACTICAL POINTS FOR RUNNING THE MEETING

Everyone will be practising the relaxation and breathing exercise by themselves and then there will be a short guided part about having a caring attitude towards ourselves.

It would help if whoever is to be coordinator both practised the exercise and read the text a day or so beforehand.

HELLO TIME

Coordinator

Allow an appropriate period of time for people to say hello and chat.

Focus the group.

Ask how everyone has got on since the last meeting.

Did anyone practise the observing and naming meditation?

Introduce today's meditation:

Is everyone OK about practising relaxation and breathing by themselves?

This will be followed by a guided part.

SETTLING DOWN

Settle down with some music.

MEDITATION PERIOD

MEDITATION

Coordinator

Use this text or lead in your own way. (For the simplified CALM course play CD from track 6.)

Sitting comfortably, let's begin.

Allow about five minutes altogether for relaxation and breathing exercises then indicate that it's time to move on.

Now we return to the level of the heart.

With each breath in we open our hearts to let in love.

After less than a minute guide meditation as follows:

Now continuing to breath gently, we focus attention back in our bodies.

Starting from the top and working down, inwardly thank each part of your body for all that it has done for you.

Guide this part initially – unhurriedly working down and identifying parts to inwardly thank and be grateful for.

Allow genuine feelings of caring and compassion to develop towards this body that tries so hard to be there for us.

(Pause for a few minutes.)

Also be aware of things you may have been struggling with . . . tensions, worries, fears.

Allow a feeling of compassionate acceptance to be present towards whatever you are experiencing.

When it feels right, invite group to have a period of silence.

Read out this quotation towards end of the silence:

Love is heaven's kindly light, the Holy Spirit's eternal breath that vivifieth the human soul. Love is the cause of God's revelation unto man, the vital bond inherent, in accordance with the divine creation, in the realities of things. Love is the one means that ensureth true felicity both in this world and the next. Love is the light that guideth in darkness, the living link that uniteth God with man, that assureth the progress of every illumined soul. Love is the most great law that ruleth this mighty and heavenly cycle, the unique power that bindeth together the divers elements of this material world, the supreme magnetic force that directeth the movements of the spheres in the celestial realms. Love revealeth with unfailing and limitless power the mysteries latent in the universe. Love is the spirit of life unto the adorned body of mankind, the establisher of true civilization in this mortal world.[21]

Allow a period for reflection then bring the meditation to a close.

Could we all bring our attention back into the room now and focus our attention on our feet resting firmly on the ground. (Give people a minute to readjust.)

CONSULTATION
FEEDBACK

Coordinator

Invite feedback about the meditation.

How easy did you find it to have caring feelings towards your body or thoughts?

Move on to study of quotations as appropriate.

Quotations

Our attitude to our personal growth and practice of meditation should be:

> *Loving:* 'We cherish the hope that through the loving-kindness of the All-Wise . . . obscuring dust may be dispelled and the power of perception enhanced . . .'[22]

> *Patient:* 'We must not only be patient with others, infinitely patient!, but also with our own poor selves . . .'[23]

> *Organic:* '. . . ye should grow in faith and constancy as day followeth day . . .'[24]

> *Moderate:* 'Whatsoever passeth beyond the limits of moderation will cease to exert a beneficial influence.'[25]

Possible Questions

Quotation 1

- How does loving kindness dispel dust when we are meditating?

Quotation 2

- In what ways do we get impatient with ourselves?
- What would be a helpful attitude to have towards ourselves when we feel we have fallen short?

Quotation 3

- How can we make our spiritual growth a natural, unforced process?

Quotation 4

- What does being moderate mean in relation to caring about ourselves?
- What does being moderate mean in relation to meditation?

CONCLUDE
Coordinator

> Anything else to share?

SOCIALIZE

To release our latent potential we need to practise meditation regularly and effectively. Regular, effective meditation will lead to growth and transformation. Transformation also means change and when we endeavour to change the ego will put up resistance. We need to learn to avoid battling with ourselves and manage resistance through a nurturing process.

Becoming aware of resistance when it arises in us is the first step in learning to manage it because awareness of the different influences within us opens up the possibility of our choosing more skilfully how we feel, think and act. The second step is to accept and acknowledge our feelings, rather than deny or minimize them. Then let the heart invite all parts of us, each seeking its cupful, to become satisfied from the vast inner ocean.

Sometimes, though, while we are practising our meditation, there may be something interesting or unpleasant that insists upon coming into our consciousness that does need attention and we need to decide, if this is the case, when is the best time to deal with it. However, as a rule of thumb, consider regarding anything that attempts to prevent, divert from or stop our regular practice as guilty of being 'resistance' until proved innocent.

Another consideration may sometimes be whether the people close to us themselves feel threatened by our efforts to change. Are there signs that they might unconsciously be trying to obstruct our practice? Is there a need to communicate what is happening with them? Do they need nurturing too?

Something else we may experience as we become more self-aware is that we will be more conscious of our shortcomings and this may make us feel that, despite our efforts, we are becoming a worse person. This is a natural consequence of our increasing self-awareness, and rather than feeling disheartened and giving up, we should redouble our efforts at nurturing the young plant of our growth. As we begin to recognize more clearly what it is in life that uplifts us we can learn to choose to let the 'Divine Spirit' help us avoid those things that bring us down.

Part of the usefulness of the 'preparatory phase' prior to meditation – when we ask ourselves, 'Why do I want to meditate?' – is that it helps to generate unity among our various inner agendas so that all parts of us can say, 'Yes, meditating would be the highest good for all of us right now.' This will, in a sense, give us permission, and make it easier, to meditate.

Here are some excuses we might use when we don't feel like changing. They seem to float up from different levels of our consciousness, depending on how much progress we are making with our spiritual journey. There may, of course, be truth in a few of these some of the time.

- I really ought to be getting on with . . .
- I'll just do this one thing before I start.
- I'm no good at it.
- The room is too hot/cold.
- I'm uncomfortable, my leg itches, my back hurts, etc.
- I don't like the lighting, the music, the incense . . .
- I've forgotten to phone . . . whoever.
- I must stop and write this down now before I forget.
- Any daydream journey our desire is taken on, that floats up from the unconscious to divert us from practice.

What are some of the thoughts that try to put you off meditating? Perhaps we could compare favourites next time we meet.

9

Bearing Fruit

Earlier in the CALM course we looked at the model of the sun and the mirror – our souls being like a mirror that can receive and reflect the light. As we evaluate our development on this journey of personal growth and fulfilment, we will find that this receiving and giving is one of the fundamental principles of the path. Though there will be times when we feel so empty that we just need to receive, like a thirsty vessel that needs filling, once we start to become restored we will find that if the spirit within us is not to become stagnant, we need to learn to become like a channel through which the living waters flow. By letting these inner spiritual resources appear in our thoughts and feelings and actions they become part of us and bear fruit for both ourselves and those around us.

What we are looking at in this coming meeting could be described as a problem-solving method for helping this to happen, for letting spirit manifest itself in action. It could, of course, be used for exploring opportunities rather than just solving problems. Part of the first step is described as 'prayer', which may mean different things to different people. For those for whom this is not a familiar part of their life, this is one way it could be viewed.

A useful analogy is that of a hydro-electric power plant in which the vast reservoir of water that is held back behind the dam is channelled down through tunnels to the turbines below that generate the electricity. If the turbines were on the same level as the top of the dam there would be no flow and so no power generated. There also needs to be a reason for the power of electricity to flow. All the electricity generated by the dam would be pointless unless someone somewhere switched something on.

In the same way we can put ourselves in the position of the turbines, in a receptive, open, empty attitude, willing to receive what assistance we need from the vast spiritual reservoir. If, in addition, there is a particular reason for us to receive and give out, it focuses the spiritual energies and makes them more effective.

In one sense this is prayer: being in the here and now and being truthful with ourselves, identifying an issue, acknowledging that we need help to deal with it and then being willing channels for the help to come through. One way that this has been described is that prayer is like talking to God and meditation is listening for the reply.

In relation to meditation, if it has a purpose, if in the lead up to it we have identified a goal, a problem, an opportunity, that we are sincerely motivated to do something about and we are willing to make ourselves receptive to help from the 'spiritual world', our meditation will become more effective. The goal could even be 'I'm confused and don't know what the goal is'. All we need to do is hold the issue, as we feel it or understand it, turn our souls to the light and wait patiently – like sitting outside waiting for the clouds to pass until the sun shines on us.

This is very similar to what we did in meeting 5 when we practised finding our own 'mantra' and, in fact, sometimes it may be useful to sum up our issue in a word or phrase and repeat it, in the same way, to help keep us focused. In a way, this type of heartfelt invocation is like repeating a short prayer – the secret is learning to allow inspiration to come and not let the mind interfere with its preconceived ideas.

This time in the meditation we will be practising something similar to what we have done before. We will focus on a particular issue and practise just staying with it, to see what thoughts and feelings come to us about it.

THE DYNAMICS OF PRAYER

This is a method for solving problems which Shoghi Effendi, the Guardian of the Bahá'í Faith, gave to Ruth Moffett, an early follower, pointing out that this is not the only method we could use.

We will be using this as a basis for our problem/opportunity-resolving exercise in our next meeting.

First Step:

> *Pray and meditate about it* . . . Then remain in the silence of contemplation for a few minutes.

Second Step:

> *Arrive at a decision and hold to this.* This decision is usually born during the contemplation. It may seem almost impossible of accomplishment but if it seems to be an answer to a prayer or a way of solving the problem, then immediately take the next step.

Third Step:

> *Have determination to carry the decision through.* Many fail here. The decision, budding into determination, is blighted and instead becomes a wish or a vague longing. When determination is born, immediately take the next step.

Fourth Step:

> *Have faith and confidence* that the power will flow through you, the right way will appear, the door will open, the right thought, the right message, the right principle, or the right book will be given to you. Have confidence, and the right thing will come to your need. Then, as you rise from prayer, take at once the fifth step.

Fifth Step:

> *Act as though it had all been answered.* Act with tireless, ceaseless energy. As you act, you, yourself, will become a magnet, which will attract more power to your being, until you become an unobstructed channel for the Divine Power to flow through you. Many pray but do not remain for the last half of the first step. Some who meditate arrive at a decision, but fail to hold it. Few have the determination to carry the decision through, and still fewer have the confidence that the right thing will come to their need. But how many remember to act as though it had all been answered? How true are these words – 'Greater than the prayer is the spirit in which it is uttered, but greater than the way it is uttered is the spirit in which it is carried out.'[26]

MAIN AIMS OF THIS MEETING

To explore one way meditation can help us to deal with challenges and opportunities.

To consider what happens with our group, if anything, now the CALM course has ended.

PRACTICAL POINTS FOR RUNNING THE MEETING

The meditation we will be practising today is about learning to let inspiration on a specific issue come through. To begin with everyone will be practising a short relaxation and breathing exercise by themselves and then there will be a guided part where we will be asked to reflect on a specific question.

Obviously we may have thought about this question before but let's just see what fresh ideas might come up about it this time.

HELLO TIME

Coordinator

> Allow an appropriate period of time for people to say hello and chat.
>
> Focus the group.
>
> Ask how everyone has got on since the last meeting.
>
>> Would anybody like to share how they got on with noticing the thoughts that try to put us off meditating?
>
> Discuss feedback about resistance.
>
> Introduce meditation, if necessary, and answer any questions.

SETTLING DOWN

Settle down with some music.

MEDITATION PERIOD

MEDITATION

Coordinator

> Use this text or lead in your own way.
>
> Begin the meditation by reading this. (For the simplified CALM course play CD from track 6. Also, ask the questions below, about the future, in the period of silence.)
>
>> Sitting comfortably, let's begin.
>
> Allow about five minutes altogether for relaxation and breathing exercises then indicate that it's time to move on.

Guide meditation as follows, posing this question:

> Could we be aware that the CALM course is coming to an end and reflect on the question 'What happens next, if anything'?

> Either for us personally or as a group, what happens next, if anything?

> Be aware of the thoughts and feelings, ideas or questions that come to mind.

> Allow ideas to arise by themselves, rather than use the mind to seek them out.

When it feels right, invite the group to have a period of silence.

Read out this quotation towards the end of period of silence:

> Have faith and confidence *that the power will flow through you, the right way will appear, the door will open, the right thought, the right message, the right principle, or the right book will be given to you. Have confidence, and the right thing will come to your need. Then* . . . Act as though it had all been answered. *Act with tireless, ceaseless energy. As you act, you, yourself, will become a magnet, which will attract more power to your being, until you become an unobstructed channel for the Divine Power to flow through you.*[27]

Allow a period for reflection then bring the meditation to a close.

> Could we all bring our attention back into the room now and focus our attention on our feet resting firmly on the ground. (Give people a minute to readjust.)

CONSULTATION
FEEDBACK

Coordinator

Initiate consultation.

Possible Questions

- Would you like to share what came up for you in the meditation?
- How do you feel about continuing to meet?
- Do you feel it would help to consolidate our personal practice if we continue meeting to support each other?
- Would it be of value to others we know in the community to run another CALM course or to have a meditation group running?
- Are there any ways we would like to develop a meditation group – such as particular areas of study?
- How have we got on as far as following the five steps goes? Did we:

  - Pray and meditate about an issue?
  - Arrive at a decision?
  - Have determination to carry the decision through?

- Have faith and confidence that the power would flow through us, the right way would appear, the right door would open?
- Act?

Coordinator

Identify any outcomes that need action and initiate the necessary steps, e.g. with regard to possible further meetings.

CONCLUDE

Invite the group to complete feedback forms now, if you think this would be helpful for you.

Thank the group for the pleasure of working together during the CALM course and give everyone an opportunity to have a final say, if they wish, before concluding.

SOCIALIZE

Hopefully you have found the CALM course beneficial and will manage to continue including some of what has been learned into your life, by yourself or with others.

Though it is an introductory course the skills that have been explored can have a profound effect on our well-being generally, to the extent that we manage to practise them.

If there are times when we do not manage to keep up the practice it may be helpful to remember something that we have been doing during the CALM course, though in a different way. When you feel that life has brought you to a point at which you recognize it would be beneficial to resume practice, don't get frustrated with yourself or beat yourself up. Just start again and again.

Eventually we get to the stage where meditation is such an important and natural part of our life we would not be without its benefits.

There is much the CALM course did not cover so hopefully your journey of discovery will carry on and continue to bring many blessings to you, and through you, into the needy world in which we live.

If you feel that you have other friends with whom you would like to set up and run this CALM course, speak about this with your coordinator who will advise you on how to obtain the relevant materials.

Appendixes

Appendix 1: Helpful Tips about Practising Meditation

MOTIVATION

With meditation, as with other things, we need to be motivated, otherwise we will not achieve our goal. When we are endeavouring to meditate, if our desire to be doing something else is greater than our desire to meditate this will hamper our efforts.

This makes the period just as we start to practise very important.

To increase our motivation a question we could inwardly ask ourselves every time before we start is 'Why am I doing this?' Is it just a habit, a ritual that I am feeling obliged to do, or is there a sense of genuine recognition that setting aside this time here and now is vital for my personal well-being, spiritual progress and for being able to cope effectively in the outside world? Identifying a heartfelt reason for wanting to meditate provides motivation and focus.

The idea of the short period of affirmation used at the beginning of meditations during the CALM course is that it brings us into the here and now by asking us to find this heartfelt reason why we wish to meditate. We are also invited to consider our intentions, whether there is anything that could be more important for our souls than what we are doing right now and, if not, putting everything else aside for now and committing ourselves to the meditation.

Another aspect to this identification of a personal affirmation is that it can also be used for refocusing when the mind wanders off into daydreams during meditation – some days our minds and emotions will be much more busy because of things that have been happening in our lives.

WHERE TO MEDITATE

Choosing, or creating, an environment that feels right can be very helpful. In some parts of the world people take their special spot with them in the form of a prayer mat. We might have a particular chair or room, somewhere out of doors or several places. Without making it a superstitious ritual, we could make the environment of our 'spot' sacred by preparing it with flowers, light or some fragrance or whatever inspires us.

Using the same spot has a psychological as well as a spiritual benefit, for we unconsciously associate this place with states of spiritual communion and our soul is anticipating them before we even begin to practise.

Having a suitable environment is also a matter of minimizing distracting interruptions. So choosing somewhere without the likelihood of disturbance by other people, with the telephone unplugged, possibly without pets in the room and so on, are things to consider. Perhaps if we live with others they could help us to have a space in the day when we could practise and we could do the same for them, especially if there are children around.

WHEN

When we are learning to meditate it is very helpful if we can find a regular time once or twice a day when we can fit practice into our often busy schedules. In addition, we can also meditate if and when we feel like it. Try out different times of the day and see how they feel.

It is not helpful to be trying to meditate if there is something else we really ought to be doing. We should be able to confirm to ourselves as we begin our practice that we are pleased, able and willing to dedicate this time now for the nourishment of our souls.

Many people find that it is not useful to try and meditate soon after a meal. Meditating after eating will have the opposite effect to fasting, as well as make it easier to fall asleep. Exercise, though, can be valuable. Some people, for instance, practise Tai Chi or yoga before meditating. Whatever exercise we do tends to make us more awake.

HOW LONG

Bearing in mind that we are learning to develop new and more helpful patterns of thinking and feeling that will, with practice, become part of us, how well we meditate is more important than how long we do so. A few minutes' effective meditation is going to benefit us more than battling through half an hour and ending up unhappy about what we've not achieved. Having said this, we could try and stretch ourselves a bit as well.

When considering how long to meditate we could take a lesson from nature. Seeds don't instantly become flowers. Through roots, shoots and leaves, they develop over seasons or years. Our growth, too, needs to be naturally nurtured, however fast or slow it may be, and after meditation we should experience an improved sense of well-being. If, after practising, we are emotionally or mentally less able to function well and cannot understand why, it would be best to stop the practice for now and seek support from whoever is running the meetings. Perhaps try starting with 10 to 20 minutes, once or twice a day and be sensitive to how you are getting on.

Having completed our meditation, rather than rushing back into the world, spending a period reflecting on what is ahead of us, and how we can be prepared to meet it, can help us to put what we feel into practice and promote unity between the spiritual and practical parts of our lives.

These are some of the practical points that can make meditation easier. However, being fanatical about everything being just right can become an obstacle in itself. It's mostly a matter of common sense and letting go.

It will help to remember these things:

- Just before you start meditating ask yourself why you are doing it (because you want to be a more joyful, peaceful, mindful being, or whatever it is) and commit yourself to it – to something that is, after all, beneficial for you.

- Learn to allow yourself just to be with, and take an interest in, the experience of the relaxation or breathing exercise.

- Once you become aware that you have become distracted by sounds around you or wandered into thoughts:

    - **identify** what you are experiencing – car sound, dog barking, thought, daydream

    - **focus** on it briefly to experience it for what it is

    - **return,** again and again, to the practice without any frustration about having become distracted

In this way everything becomes part of the meditation rather than working against it.

Appendix 2: Chart of a Session Using the Simplified Format

Hello Time	Say hello and settle down.	Unchanged
Meditation Period	Play guided meditation track of CD.	Remember to read the specified passage towards the end of the silent period.
Consultation	Invite feedback from meditation. Read quotations and share thoughts. Use the questions if they help.	Some of the suggested feedback questions may be irrelevant when just using the CD.
Socialize		Unchanged

Appendix 3: Optional Feedback Form for Participants

What did you like most about the CALM course?

What did you like least about the CALM course?

What could be done to improve it?

Do you feel that the CALM course has helped you to have a rewarding experience of meditation?

If yes, how would you describe it?

Do you think the CALM course provides enough information about how to meditate for you to be able to continue practising by yourself?

If not, in what way could it be improved?

Was the *CALM Handbook* helpful?

How could it be improved?

Do you intend to continue practising by yourself?

Would you like to continue meeting with other people to meditate?

Appendix 4: Key Figures and Institutions of the Bahá'í Faith

The quotations and other writings cited in the *CALM Coordinator's Guide* and the *CALM Handbook* are from the Bahá'í teachings. For those not familiar with the Bahá'í Faith, this brief synopsis of the key figures whose works are quoted might be helpful.

BAHÁ'U'LLÁH

Bahá'u'lláh is the prophet-founder of the Bahá'í Faith. Bahá'ís believe He is the great teacher from God for this day. 'Bahá'u'lláh' is a title, meaning the 'Glory of God'. His writings, along with those of His forerunner, the Báb, and His son, 'Abdu'l-Bahá, constitute the sacred scriptures of the Bahá'í Faith.

Bahá'u'lláh was born Mírzá Ḥusayn 'Alí on 12 November 1817 to a noble family in Iran. He became a follower of the Báb in 1844 and eventually became a leader of the Bábí community. He was imprisoned for four months in an underground prison in Tehran known as the Síyáh-Chál. There He received a revelation of His mission. He was banished from Iran and went to Baghdad with His family and companions. After ten years there and as He was preparing to leave, Bahá'u'lláh declared His mission publicly in the Garden of Riḍván in April and May 1863. Bahá'u'lláh was sent from place to place and was finally imprisoned in 'Akká in the west of the Ottoman Empire, where He died in 1892.

Bahá'u'lláh wrote many letters and epistles, including to the kings and rulers of His day, proclaiming His mission to bring about the recognition of the oneness of humanity and to establish universal peace.

THE BÁB

The Báb was the forerunner of Bahá'u'lláh and the prophet-founder of the Bábí religion. His writings are considered to be part of the sacred scriptures of the Bahá'í Faith.

The 'Báb' is a title that means the 'Gate'. The Báb was born Siyyid 'Alí-Muḥammad on 20 October 1819 in Shiraz, Iran. In May 1844 He declared Himself to be the Promised One of Islam, stating that His mission was to announce the imminent advent of another great teacher, 'Him whom God shall make manifest'. Many people followed Him, alarming the clergy. The Báb was imprisoned, tried and sentenced to die before a firing squad. On 9 July 1850, a firing squad of 750 rifles shot at the Báb but He was unharmed. Afterwards the Báb was found back in His cell, finishing a conversation with His secretary. He was brought before a new firing squad and this time was executed, along with a companion. After 50 years His remains were brought to Mount Carmel in the Holy Land, where they were interred.

'ABDU'L-BAHÁ

'Abdu'l-Bahá was born 'Abbás Effendi and was the eldest surviving son of Bahá'u'lláh. His father designated 'Abdu'l-Bahá to be His successor and the authorized interpreter of His writings. 'Abdu'l-Bahá's writings are part of the sacred scriptures of the Bahá'í Faith. The title "Abdu'l-Bahá' means 'Servant of the Glory'.

'Abdu'l-Bahá spent 55 years as a prisoner and an exile. When Bahá'u'lláh passed away, 'Abdu'l-Bahá became the head of the Bahá'í Faith. He wrote many letters to individuals and to Bahá'í communities explaining the religion and its teachings. After His release from prison in 'Akká in 1908, He travelled to the West to help spread the religion. He spoke to many individuals, and societies, including churches, women's groups and workers' unions, about the teachings brought by His father, especially the need to establish peace. His talks are not Bahá'í scripture but give important insights into the teachings of Bahá'u'lláh. 'Abdu'l-Bahá was the perfect example of how a Bahá'í should live. He passed away on 28 November 1921.

SHOGHI EFFENDI

Shoghi Effendi was born in 'Akká in 1897 and was the great-grandson of Bahá'u'lláh. He was appointed by 'Abdu'l-Bahá in His Will and Testament to be the Guardian of the Bahá'í Faith and, like his grandfather, the interpreter of the Bahá'í scripture. He was educated at the American University at Beirut and at Balliol College, Oxford.

He was a young man studying in Oxford when his grandfather, 'Abdu'l-Bahá, passed away and he learned that he had been appointed Guardian. During his ministry the Bahá'í Faith developed and grew and was spread to all parts of the globe. Shoghi Effendi established the Bahá'í governing system, clarified many aspects of the Bahá'í teachings and, through his many letters, guided the emerging world community. He translated numerous passages from the writings of Bahá'u'lláh, wrote a lengthy history of the Bahá'í Faith, developed the Bahá'í World Centre and supervised the building of the Shrine of the Báb and the International Archives Building on Mount Carmel. He passed away in London on 5 November 1957 and is buried there.

THE UNIVERSAL HOUSE OF JUSTICE

In His Book of Laws, Bahá'u'lláh established the Universal House of Justice as the supreme administrative body of the Bahá'í Faith. It was elected for the first time in 1963 and is the head of the Bahá'í Faith. The Universal House of Justice has a number of powers and duties, including the enactment of laws and ordinances not expressly set out in the Bahá'í scriptures. It consults about and makes decisions on a variety of issues, elucidates obscure questions and is charged with safeguarding the personal rights, freedom and initiative of individuals. The Universal House of Justice is elected every five years.

BIBLIOGRAPHY

'Abdu'l-Bahá. *Paris Talks*. London: Bahá'í Publishing Trust, 1967.
— *The Promulgation of Universal Peace*. Wilmette, IL: Bahá'í Publishing Trust, 1982.
— *Selections from the Writings of 'Abdu'l-Bahá*. Haifa: Bahá'í World Centre, 1978.
The Báb. *Selections from the Writings of the Báb*. Haifa: Bahá'í World Centre, 1976.
Bahá'í Prayers: A Selection of Prayers revealed by Bahá'u'lláh, the Báb and 'Abdu'l-Bahá. Wilmette, IL: Bahá'í Publishing Trust, 2002.
Bahai Scriptures. New York: Brentano's, 1923.
Bahá'u'lláh. *Gleanings from the Writings of Bahá'u'lláh*. Wilmette, IL: Bahá'í Publishing Trust, 1983.
— *The Hidden Words*. Wilmette, IL: Bahá'í Publishing Trust, 1990.
— *Tablets of Bahá'u'lláh*. Wilmette, IL: Bahá'í Publishing Trust, 1988.
The Compilation of Compilations. Prepared by the Universal House of Justice 1963–1990. 2 vols. [Mona Vale NSW]: Bahá'í Publications Australia, 1991.
Moffett, Ruth. *Du'á: On Wings of Prayer*. Happy Camp, CA: Naturegraph Publishers, rev. edn. 1984.
Oxford English Dictionary.
Shoghi Effendi. *The Unfolding Destiny of the British Bahá'í Community: The Messages of the Guardian of the Bahá'í Faith to the Bahá'ís of the British Isles*. London: Bahá'í Publishing Trust, 1981.
The Universal House of Justice. Letter to the Bahá'ís of the World, 28 December 1999.

ENDNOTES

1. 'Abdu'l-Bahá, *Paris Talks*, pp. 175–6.
2. ibid. p. 175.
3. ibid. p. 176.
4. ibid. p. 175.
5. ibid.
6. *Oxford English Dictionary*
7. 'Abdu'l-Bahá, *Promulgation*, pp. 147–8.
8. ibid.
9. Bahá'u'lláh, *Gleanings*, pp. 65–6.
10. *Oxford English Dictionary*
11. 'Abdu'l-Bahá, *Selections*, pp. 110–11.
12. ibid. p. 176.
13. The Báb, *Selections*, pp. 93–4.
14. ibid.
15. *Oxford English Dictionary*
16. Bahá'u'lláh, *Gleanings*, pp. 259–60.
17. ibid.
18. From a letter written on behalf of Shoghi Effendi, 16 October 1926, in *Unfolding Destiny*, pp. 422–3.
19. 'Abdu'l-Bahá, *Bahai Scriptures*, p. 546.
20. 'Abdu'l-Bahá, *Paris Talks*, p. 175.
21. 'Abdu'l-Bahá, *Selections*, p. 27.
22. Bahá'u'lláh, *Tablets*, p. 35.
23. From a letter written on behalf of Shoghi Effendi, 22 October 1949, in *Unfolding Destiny*, p. 456.
24. 'Abdu'l-Bahá, *Selections*, p. 19.
25. Bahá'u'lláh, *Gleanings*, p. 216.
26. Moffett, *Du'á*, p. 28.
27. ibid.

Guided Meditation CD

This recorded guided meditation is intended to accompany the course, using the relevant tracks as necessary, until participants feel confident to practise without it.

MUSIC

Track 1	Create in Me	4'33"
	Composed and performed by Michaela and Geoff Smith	
Track 2	Breezes of Eternity (part)	4'34"
	Composed and performed by Malcolm Dedman	
Track 3	Interlude	1'59"
	Composed and performed by Michaela and Geoff Smith	
Track 4	Inner Sanctuary	12'58"
	Composed and performed by Malcolm Dedman	

GUIDED MEDITATION

Track 5	Introduction	4'28"
Track 6	Affirmation and Commitment	1'41"
Track 7	Relaxation	4'00"
Track 8	Breathing	9'03"
Track 9	Attunement	10'54"

Paul Profaska

was introduced to meditation when he became a Bahá'í and has found it an indispensable source of inspiration, comfort and strength over the last 30 years. For much of this time he has been involved in creating opportunities, through workshops and groups, for people to explore the benefits of meditation and gain insights into its principles.

In 1999 he coordinated a pilot project for the National Spiritual Assembly of the Bahá'ís of the United Kingdom to promote the use of meditation in a way that would be acceptable to people from all backgrounds. The CALM course is the outcome of that project.

Geoff and Michaela Smith

live in Cornwall, United Kingdom. In between working and raising their musical family of four they find time and energy to perform locally, often using their own compositions, Michaela captures the spirit of the Bahá'í writings and life events in the songs she composes, and Geoff does the arrangements in their small studio. The music on this CD is taken from their albums 'Ancient Beauty' and 'Traces' and is reproduced here by their kind permission.

Malcolm Dedman

(b. 1948) has been writing music since the age of 12. His first formal composition lessons were with Patric Stanford at the Guildhall School of Music and Drama in 1972. Although influenced by many 20th century composers, Malcolm believes in writing music that speaks directly to the audience, has a purposeful message to convey, in a style that is appropriate to this century and without compromising musical quality. The music on this CD is taken from his album 'Tranquillity Zone', music for relaxation, meditation and peace, and is reproduced here by his kind permission.